What People Are Saying...

"Thank you so much for your devotionals, which are the best I have ever read... Your devotionals are so fresh and inspiring, as well as challenging, without being condemning. Some devotionals can make people feel inadequate or unworthy. Yours are encouraging and upbuilding. I pray ADONAI will bless you in your ministry. Thank you once again." –H.A., United Kingdom

"I continue to be amazed at the direct personal relevance of your Daily Devotional. This is just to say 'thank you' again for your ministry, which is so obviously gifted by our G-d." –H.L., Northern Ireland

"I can't express what a blessing the devotionals are in my life. The prayers seem to reach down deep in my heart and pull out the words I feel, and often tears flow with joy. The subjects seem to be perfect [for] what my spirit needs. You are truly a blessing. Thank you!" –J.J., USA

"I just wanted to say thank you. Your devotionals minister to me regularly. I subscribe to many different ones, but I can honestly say that your devotionals have spoken directly to issues that I have needed to hear on more than any other that I have read. I can't begin to express how truly grateful I am that you allow the Messiah Yeshua to use you in this way as the truths that you espouse speak directly to my soul in a way that so many others haven't. Again, thank you, and may our Lord's blessings upon you be many." –M.V., USA

"If I sent you a note every time one of the devotionals ministered to my heart, you would be receiving *lots* of notes from me! I just thank ADONAI for the faithful words and insights He is communicating through you. Thank you for sitting at Yeshua's feet and hearing His Words of life, then passing them on to us." –L.R., USA

"Todah! My wife and I… appreciate the beautiful fruit that comes to us through your daily devotionals. We are deeply indebted and you encourage us daily. We will continue to pray for you as you feed the many." –E.D., USA

"I suppose people say this to you all the time—I know the ones I know feel as I do—your devotional is so often just exactly what I needed… so on target for that day and hour. May the joy we receive from His work through you abound in *your* life and of those you love." –C.A., USA

"I just want to thank you so much for your anointed devotionals… my heart thrills when I see that my next devotional has arrived in my email!! Are you considering a devotional book? I would so love to share these with other people. Thank you for your service and ministry. I am one who is hearing from the Lord, through you, His vessel." –J.M., USA

"After forty-five years of walking with the Lord, I've read *lots* of devotionals. Yours are by far, the most anointed, insightful, and rewarding I've ever had the pleasure to read. Gather them all together and publish a book of these wonderful life-giving words coming through *you* from the Spirit of Yeshua!" –K.S., USA

MESSIANIC *Daily* DEVOTIONAL

KEVIN GEOFFREY

PERFECT *Word*
P·U·B·L·I·S·H·I·N·G

A ministry of Perfect Word Ministries

P · U · B · L · I · S · H · I · N · G

A ministry of Perfect Word Ministries

PO Box 82954 • Phoenix, AZ 85071
www.PerfectWordMinistries.org
1-888-321-PWMI

All Scripture quotations are from *The Holy Bible Consisting of The Old and New Covenants Translated According to the Letter and Idioms of the Original Languages (Young's Literal Translation) by Robert Young, LL.D.*, which is in the public domain. Archaic English words such as "thee" and "thou" have been updated. Where deemed appropriate, other words and phrases were re-rendered using the original texts. Updating for the modern Messianic reader is ©2006-2010 by Perfect Word Ministries, Inc.

ISBN #: 0-9785504-0-4

Printed in the United States of America

וְהָיָה לְבַבְכֶם שָׁלֵם עִם יהוה אֱלֹהֵינוּ
לָלֶכֶת בְּחֻקָּיו וְלִשְׁמֹר מִצְוֹתָיו כַּיּוֹם הַזֶּה

"And [may] your heart be perfect[ly devoted]
to ADONAI our God, to walk in His statutes
and to keep His commandments as at this day."

מְלָכִים א M'lachiym Alef (1Kings) 8:61

Preface

For many years—since 1999, in fact—the *Messianic Daily Devotional* has been a part of my life. It has been a focal point for my own personal quality time in the Word as often as it has been a stinging reminder of my lack thereof.

I have often struggled with the usefulness of this thing we call a "daily devotional," wondering if writing —much less reading—one was worth anyone's time. All too often, we as disciples of Messiah settle for "nuggets" of truth and become easily moved by "new revelation" from the Word. I have mused, therefore, that a daily devotional may not be useful at all—perhaps it merely serves to enable an immature faith among shallow followers of a distant Messiah.

But somewhere along the way, I became a believer —in the usefulness of a daily devotional, that is. E-mail after e-mail, one encouraging note after another, I began to see a pattern in the lives of my readers: slowly but surely, their lives were being changed. And finally, I believed. I believed that there was a special message that ADONAI wanted to communicate through these little daily devotionals. I realized that the purpose of this daily devotional was to help grow mature and useful disciples of Messiah.

The *Messianic Daily Devotional* is not just some insightful collection of Messianic Bible commentaries, nor is it a grouping of revelatory morsels intended to make you feel all warm and fuzzy inside. The *Messianic Daily Devotional* is an effective tool for turning over fertile soil in the lives of both new and seasoned believers —so that together we can grow and be strengthened in the way we are devoted to God... daily.

Thank you for allowing me to walk with you each day as we continue to follow in the footsteps of our Master. As you make this book part of your daily devotions to God, I pray that the Scriptures contained herein will captivate and draw you; that their corresponding devotional writings will spark in you a fresh understanding of the Scriptures; and that as you begin to pray in accordance with the Word of God, the Spirit will lead you into a time of deep and meaningful devotion, worship and praise that will change your life—today, forever, and for good.

In Yeshua,

Kevin Geoffrey
May 21, 2006

Introduction

In 1999, the *Messianic Daily Devotional* began as an e-mail devotional from one of the longest-running Messianic Jewish websites in Internet history—*MessiahNet.com*. At that time, simply being an e-mail devotional was relatively unique, but what continually set these devotionals apart was their distinctly Messianic Jewish point of view. It is important to note, however, that these devotionals are not designed to be a resource for learning about Messianic Jewish theology or practices. In fact, we have purposely avoided a teaching style intended to impart *information*, and instead opted for a personal style designed to encourage *devotion*. Time and again, this approach has been affirmed by our readers, as they consistently comment that these devotionals are unlike any they have ever read.

This volume contains brand new devotionals, as well as newly edited versions of some of our best e-mail devotionals. When we began compiling this book, we found that even though time has passed since some of the devotionals were first written, they still have a powerful and encouraging message for us today. Over the years, these writings have been a blessing to Jews and Gentiles, men and women, laymen and leaders—and we hope that this newest version of the *Messianic Daily Devotional* will minister to the Body of Messiah in greater ways than ever before.

Features

All of the devotionals in this book begin with a passage of Scripture, upon which the devotional writing is based.

These are not teachings or commentaries on the passage, but are exhortative writings that are intended to encourage discipleship and devotion to God. Each devotional concludes with a suggested prayer that will help give you a "jump-start" as you enter into a time of fellowship with ADONAI.

Most of the devotionals contain "restored" Hebrew names and places, the most obvious of which are Yeshua (rendered in most English translations of the Bible as "Jesus"), and Messiah (rendered in most English translations as "Christ"). This "restoration" was done for several reasons. First, it serves as a reminder of the Hebraic nature of our Scriptures—and how often they can be truly foreign to our western-thinking minds. Second, it demonstrates the ongoing and perpetual Jewishness of our faith and our Messiah. Finally, it helps to increase our familiarity with and love for the Hebrew language —the native tongue of the nation of Israel, and of her promised redeemer, Yeshua.

Not wishing to trivialize the use of Hebrew within a book written for an English-speaking audience, we have gone a step beyond simply embedding *transliterated*[1] Hebrew. In passages of Scripture that were originally written in Hebrew, we have also included the actual Hebrew letters with their *nikudot* (vowel marks or vowel points).[2] This should be especially beneficial for those who are just beginning to learn the Hebrew language. In some cases, we have included the *translated*[3] English

---

[1] A transliteration is a phonetic representation of words from another language. For instance, "Yeshua" is an English transliteration of the Hebrew, יֵשׁוּעַ.
[2] Most of the vowel sounds in Hebrew are not represented by letters of the *alef-beit*, but instead have been preserved for posterity through the vowel-pointing system of the *nikudot*.
[3] A translation gives the *meaning* of a word, while transliteration gives only its *pronunciation*.

word just after the restored Hebrew and transliteration. However, a reverse glossary—alphabetized according to the transliterated English—is also provided at the back of the book, enabling the reader to look up the meaning of each Hebrew word used in the devotionals.

The Sacred Name

For the sake of brevity, there are two familiar Hebrew words used throughout the devotionals that are rendered with transliteration *alone*—Yeshua and Adonai.[4] However, when the word "ADONAI" is printed with all capital letters, it actually represents a *different* word altogether: יהוה, the "Sacred Name" of God.[5]

So why don't we use an English transliteration to help us pronounce the Sacred Name? The reason is that we simply do not know how to properly pronounce it. According to Jewish tradition, the Name is not to be spoken aloud, out of proper respect for the Holy One. Whenever the Scriptures were read aloud, the reader would speak "Adonai," rather than uttering the Name itself. Thus, when the Jewish scribes were adding the *nikudot* to the Scriptures, they purposely superimposed the *nikudot* for אֲדֹנָי, *Adonai* upon the Name in order to remind the reader to make the appropriate substitution. With time, the pronunciation of the Name was lost—or at least obscured beyond recovery.

Though some scholars and other individuals maintain that the pronunciation of the Name has indeed been preserved from antiquity—or can be reasonably discerned

---

[4] A title for God, meaning "Lord" or "Master."
[5] In English, this name is sometimes represented as YHWH or YHVH, the English letters which correspond to the four Hebrew letters of The Name.

from what we know of Hebrew—it is *our* belief that this is just not so. Therefore, with no confidence in the accuracy of any given pronunciation, we have opted to represent יהוה with "ADONAI," in keeping with the tradition. Where יהוה appears next to אֲדֹנָי, *Adonai* in the text, the name that is rendered with capital letters is the one used to represent the Sacred Name, i.e. *Adonai ELOHIYM.*[6]

Young's Literal Translation of the Holy Bible (1862/1898) by Robert Young

One of the challenges in devotional writing—or any kind of Bible teaching, for that matter—is avoiding personal "inspiration" or "revelation" sparked solely from the English translation. When a teacher relies exclusively on a specific translation, he risks having a distorted view of the text, or even missing its point altogether.

Although translators do their best to retain the meanings of the original text, there is always some linguistic work and paraphrasing based on the translator's understanding. While some Bible translations take more liberty than others, their goal is generally to make the Scriptures more readable for the new audience—and a translation that is more readable is therefore more meaningful. While this approach is helpful in communicating ideas and concepts, such alterations unavoidably add to or change the meaning of a passage when it is read subjectively.

In an attempt to compensate for the skewed "inspiration" that can come from reading English translations, we chose to work with the *Young's Literal Translation.*

---

[6] The Hebrew אֱלֹהִים, *Elohiym* (and occasionally אֵל, *El*) is usually translated in English as "God." Where the word "God" appears in the devotional Scripture passages originally from the Hebrew, it is translating this word.

First published in 1862, this "literal" translation attempts to retain direct one-to-one word translations, word order, colloquialisms, and literal phrase renderings from the original language. As you can imagine, this makes for a sometimes dramatically different reading from other English translations. Despite this advantage, however, the "old English" style of the text is often cumbersome, making it very difficult to use at times.

Thankfully, another aspect of the *Young's* worked in our favor—the translation is in the public domain, and therefore free from copyright. As such, we had the freedom to work with the text, bringing the language into 21st century North American English. We were also able to restore the Hebrew names of people and places, along with other words which we felt worked better in the original language. As we made these updates, we were constantly forced to go back to the original languages, as well as making comparisons with various other English translations. In the end, we arrived at a fresh, meaningful, and hopefully accurate translation.

Although every attempt was made to keep the translation as literal as possible, there were some instances where additional English words were necessary. Where Young added words not in the original language, they are set off from the italicized Scriptures as normal text. Where *we* added words that were neither in the *Young's* nor in the original text, they are set off by brackets. These words were added to make for a smooth, unencumbered reading of the passage—but in most cases, you will find that they can be read and under-stood without our bracketed embellishments.

Hey! Where's The Torah?

You may have noticed that there is one glaring omission from this *Messianic Daily Devotional* book.

Where are the devotionals based on passages from the Torah? Be assured—we do have Torah devotionals!

When we look at the Scriptures, we find that the Torah itself has a devotional nature. Israel is to have Torah's *"words... on your heart,"* [7] and King David says that Torah is the happy man's *"delight, and in [ADONAI's] Torah he will meditate by day and by night."* [8]

With this in mind, we felt that the Torah deserved special attention as a devotional source. As a result, the *Messianic Torah Devotional* book (August, 2008) is based solely on passages from the five books of Moshe. This separate and unique volume contains extended devotionals for each of the fifty-four Torah portions, as delineated by the traditional Jewish annual reading schedule. If the *Messianic Daily Devotional* is a blessing to you, we believe you will find the *Messianic Torah Devotional* to be a delight!

The Daily Discipline of Devotion

Each of us is in a different stage of life, with varying responsibilities, pressures, and other demands on our time and energy. As disciples of Messiah, however, we cannot afford to allow *life* to dictate how we *live*. The only way we can ever hope to gain control over our lives is to yield ourselves completely to God. Though we may prefer it to be otherwise, such surrender is not a one-time event—it is ongoing, and requires a daily commitment. Undying devotion to God is key to living an effective, useful, *and happy* life for Messiah.

One way to begin developing that daily discipline of devotion is through the use of devotional resources such

---

[7] Deuteronomy 6:6
[8] Psalm 1:2

as the *Messianic Daily Devotional.* Though you may find the writings to be inspirational and useful for sharpening you as a believer in Yeshua, the *Messianic Daily Devotional* is only intended to be a starting place for what we pray will be a meaningful and ever-deepening devotional life.

The following are just a few practical suggestions for how to incorporate the *Messianic Daily Devotional* into your life, as you continually develop that daily discipline of devotion.

Examples of Ways to Use the Devotional Book

❖ In private devotions—to spark your relationship with ADONAI

❖ During family devotions—to begin a time of prayer, discussion, or study

❖ As a discipleship tool—to help new believers get into the Word and begin to develop a daily discipline of devotion

❖ Between accountability partners—to read together or apart; to discuss or share insights for relationship building; and to keep you accountable in your daily devotions

Goals to Consider for Your Daily Devotions

❖ Set aside a special time daily to be alone with God—consider Yeshua's pattern according to Mark 1:35.

❖ Read a devotional each day, but don't forget the Scriptures! Remember, each devotional Scripture passage is but a small fragment of a larger book and chapter.

❖ Pray! Rather than *concluding* your devotional time with the prayers we have provided, use them to jump-start your time with ADONAI.

❖ Consider ways to extend your devotional time— for example, put on your favorite praise and worship music and see what happens!

This is *devotion*: to devote ourselves fully to our God, to give our lives over to Him completely, and to be captivated by the gravity and grace of His presence, so that *"in Him, we [will] live, and move, and be..."*[9]

---

[9] Acts 17:28

MESSIANIC *Daily* DEVOTIONAL

Remembering the Word of God

"…and blessed is she who believed, for there will be a completion to the things spoken to her from ADONAI." Luke 1:45

How often we forget the words of ADONAI and miss the blessing! Thankfully, He continues in His faithfulness toward us even when our memories fail. Distracted by the troubles and challenges of life, we forget His word, leaving us with no basis for trust. This is right where the enemy wants us—distracted to the point of forgetting. If only we could remember….

The breakdown is in our daily devotions—our time spent listening to the things spoken to us by ADONAI. Having a deteriorating devotional life is like slowly starving to death. In the beginning, you experience a period of distracting, consuming hunger when all you can think about is *eating*. But eventually, the desire to eat subsides—almost to the point that you forget you are hungry. Weak, sluggish and unproductive, you don't even realize that the source of your lethargy is a lack of fuel. You need to be fed, but you have forgotten… forgotten what it's like to *eat*.

Many of us as disciples of Messiah are in this same condition in our spiritual lives—our walk with ADONAI has become a dirge, and we can't seem to put our finger on why we feel so detached from and abandoned by God. This is because somewhere along the line, we started slacking off on our prayer time, our private devotions, fellowship with other healthy believers, hearing the preaching or teaching of the Word, entering into the presence of God through praise and worship, giving thanks in all circumstances, both good and bad, and on and on.... Without the daily renewal and nourishment through the promises of God, we wither and shrivel—slowly, so that we barely notice—and become ineffective servants for the Master.

But be encouraged! ADONAI is forever faithful. His blessings await us when we renew our trust in Him. Revive your passion, find your first love, and He will show you the completion of all He has spoken. There is nothing more crucial, more vital, than the nourishment that comes from the Word of God. Be disciplined and seek ADONAI, and He will return a renewed heart, direction in life, and an outpouring of abundant blessings.

In order to receive the blessings, sometimes we have to feast even when we're not hungry—and it just might remind us that we've been starving to death.

ॐ ◌

Abba Father, renew my mind and revive my soul; remind my heart of Your faithfulness—the promises You will never take back. I give myself to You all over again; I want to feast on Your Word and receive the blessings that await me. Your grace is abundant, and I am safe in Your arms. Nourish me with Your love and help me to never forget....

Sun, Stand Still

"Then יְהוֹשֻׁעַ, *Y'hoshua spoke to* ADONAI *in the day* ADONAI *gave up the* אֱמֹרִי, *'Emori before the sons of* יִשְׂרָאֵל, *Yis'rael; and* יְהוֹשֻׁעַ, *Y'hoshua said, before the eyes of* יִשְׂרָאֵל, *Yis'rael, 'Sun—in* גִּבְעוֹן, *Giv'on stand still; and moon —in the valley of* אַיָּלוֹן, *Ayalon;' and the sun stood still, and the moon stayed—till the nation took vengeance on its enemies. Is it not written in the Book of the Upright, 'and the sun stood in the midst of the heavens, and has not made haste to go in—as a perfect day?' And there has not been [another day] like that day before it or after it, for* ADONAI's *hearing of the voice of a man; for* ADONAI *is fighting for* יִשְׂרָאֵל, *Yis'rael."* יְהוֹשֻׁעַ *Y'hoshua (Joshua) 10:12-14*

Y'hoshua had an advantage in warfare that we don't seem to have today—he was able to see not only his enemies, but also the physical manifestation of God's provision. He expected total success because he put the presence of God before him in every battle. But today, it seems our true enemy is hidden—not seen with the naked eye—and we have to take God's word for it when He says the enemy is defeated.

So, has God stopped being God? Does He still fight on behalf of His people? Will He still perform supernatural feats that will cause His people to enter into victory? And if so, can we still expect Him to hear the voice of a man? Indeed, who has faith to believe they can speak to ADONAI saying, *"Sun... stand still,"* and it will be?

The truth is that Y'hoshua operated in a greater degree of faith than many of us do today. Though he could see his enemies, it did not diminish his faith in the unseen. On the contrary, the intensity of the physical manifestation was directly related to the amount of faith Y'hoshua put in ADONAI. Y'hoshua had no faith in the people of Yis'rael, his own abilities, or the inabilities of his enemies—Y'hoshua's faith was in God alone.

The Word of God is available to us to remind us of what ADONAI is capable of and willing to do. But sometimes, our faith needs to go beyond what we *know* God can do—what we know He's done in the past—and trust Him to do something that we haven't ever seen. For Yis'rael, *"there has not been [another day] like that day before it or after it."* Today, the Lord wants to do something for you—something that *"has not been"* before today. ADONAI is hearing the voice of a man—you—and He wants to fight on your behalf. Are you prepared for your faith to grow where it *"has not been"* before?

ॐ ৵

ADONAI, I praise Your Holy Name! Only You can make the sun rise and set, and even stop in mid-air. God of Heaven and earth, prepare me to have faith like Y'hoshua's faith—the kind of faith that can say, *"Sun... stand still,"* and expect it to be so. Teach me to seek Your supernatural provision, and to broaden my mind to expect even that which I have never seen. Thank You, Abba Father, for Your creative response to my little faith. Build me up, that I may put my whole trust only in You....

By the Hand

"From ADONAI are the steps of a man,
They have been prepared, And his way he
desires. When he falls, he is not cast down,
For ADONAI holds him up by the hand."
תְּהִלִּם *T'hillim (Psalms) 37:23-24*

The paradox of life: ADONAI directs, but it is the person who steps. We are guided, yet we make the decision to move of our own accord. God has a plan for us, and the finish is predetermined from the beginning. Yet the end is not fixed—we make choices to follow or to stray. Who can reconcile such thoughts? To whom is this mystery revealed?

As we walk in the God-directed path, we desire it— it is a joy to follow the road so plainly laid out before us. Some may believe that pure freedom is the ability to go one's own way—to do as one pleases—and find "happiness" in this self-centered pursuit. But true freedom is adherence to the path—freedom from destruction, loss, pain and suffering without reason. Joy comes not from the freedom that brings autonomy, but from the freedom that brings deliverance.

In Yeshua, there will be times of stumbling—stumbling as a result of sin, or stumbling as a result of spiritual attack. But if our momentum is moving forward—not straying to the right or the left, standing still, or moving back the way we came—we won't fall into a position from which there is no recovery. If we are moving forward when we stumble, we will continue to move forward—indeed, we will hardly miss a beat.

/ *"For ADONAI holds him up by the hand,"* keeping us upright, not letting our head hit the ground. And, again, we are back to the beginning—He does the directing, we do the stepping. Sometimes He goes ahead, holding our hand out before us. Other times He is beside us, walking hand-in-hand, like a Father with His son. Sometimes He is behind us, cultivating discipline by not allowing us to go too fast and lose control. Other times He stands still, holding tight as we explore places we truly ought not to go. /

But no matter what, our hand is always held.

ও ও

Thank You, Father, for putting me on the path and teaching me to desire Your way. Thank You for keeping me from falling, and for never letting me out of Your reach. Show me, ADONAI, how to look to You when I stumble, to see how You are protecting me. You give me freedom to make mistakes; but, full of grace, You are always ready to pull me out of trouble. Teach me, Father, how to walk safely in Your ways, to be delighted in the fullness of You, and to turn back to You quickly when I've gone a little too far....

On the Mountain

"And צְבָאוֹת יהוה, ADONAI *Tz'vaot has made, for all the peoples on this mountain, a banquet of rich things, a banquet of aged wines, rich things full of marrow, refined wines. And on this mountain He will swallow up the face of the covering that is covered over all the peoples, and of the veil that is spread over all the nations. He will swallow up death in victory, and* אֲדֹנָי יהוה, *Adonai* ELOHIYM *will wipe the tears from off all faces, and the shame of His people He [will] turn aside from off all the earth, for* ADONAI *has spoken. And one will say in that day, 'Behold, this is our God, we waited for Him, and He saved us. This is* ADONAI, *we have waited for Him, we are joyful and rejoice in His salvation.' For the hand of* ADONAI *will rest on this mountain…"* יְשַׁעְיָהוּ *Y'sha'yahu (Isaiah) 25:6-10*

As disciples of the Messiah Yeshua, our most blessed salvation awaits us. ADONAI will accomplish all these great things, and we will be the recipients. But one thing will keep us from the delicious food and superb wines; one thing will obstruct the wiping away of our tears; one thing stands between us and our salvation—we must first be "on the mountain."

We are all on different legs of the journey to get to the mountain of ADONAI. In order to be on the mountain, perhaps some of us need to have more faith—to trust that ADONAI is who He says He is and will do what He has promised He will do. Perhaps others of us need to be more devoted to God—to rededicate ourselves to Him because we have been slowly slipping away. We've been seeing Him less and less in our daily lives, yet needing Him more and more.

Still others of us may need to have our mindsets changed on some things—perhaps we've been reluctant to accept the Lord's teachings and instructions on certain issues in our lives. Today is the day to trust ADONAI's voice over our own wisdom. And for still others, perhaps getting to the mountain requires us to accept God's precious gift of salvation once and for all—to stop beating ourselves up because we think we're not worthy, and to receive Yeshua as the final atonement for every last sin.

The mountain is waiting, and ADONAI will certainly meet us there. Perhaps the reason we feel that we have *"waited for Him"* so long is because, all along, He has been waiting for us to get out of the way and allow Him to bring us to the mountain....

۽ ঋ

ADONAI, You are my God. I exalt You; I praise Your name, for You have done wonderful things.... Show me where I am not making enough room for You—in my heart and in my actions. Teach me to empty myself—to be a willing vessel, that You may pour Yourself into me. ADONAI, help me to keep moving along the path You have laid out for me. I receive Your blessings, Your gifts, and the call You have placed on my life—uncover my face, wipe away my tears, save me, and take me to the mountain....

Brokenness

"Everyone who falls on that stone will be broken [to pieces], but [if that stone] falls on [him], it will crush him to powder." Luke 20:18

We often think of brokenness as the condition in which we are left after the world has had its way with us—that we come to Yeshua broken, asking Him to put us back together. After we have allowed the world to break us, we come to the Master with a pile of pieces that have been broken by human hands, hoping He can reform them. But this is not the type of brokenness the Master desires for us—in fact, He wants to be the One who does the breaking. When we allow *Yeshua* to break us, the pieces are formed by *His* hands, and we cannot dictate the pattern with which we will be reconstructed.

We are all going to fall at some time or another. So here is the question: when we fall, are we going to be *on* the stone or *under* it? When we fall, do we want the Lord to be able to pick us up again, or will we be completely annihilated? When we fall, are we falling to our knees in reverence and worship, or are we falling from heights reached by our own self-exaltation?

Everyone will eventually fall because of Yeshua. Those who fall upon the stone in humility—they will be broken to pieces and transformed into a vessel of honor. But those who erect themselves and reject the cornerstone—their kingdoms will fall and become dust.

What does it mean to be truly broken? Brokenness is being on your knees before the Lord, even when it starts to get a little uncomfortable. Brokenness is spreading out your arms, exposing your heart, looking up toward Heaven, and saying, "I'm available." Brokenness is standing naked and still in the midst of your circumstances while proclaiming, "ADONAI is my shepherd, I do not lack..." Brokenness is praising God, even when you don't feel like it. Brokenness is hearing the Holy Spirit... and not putting up a fight.

ર૭ ન૭

Abba Father, I have become rigid and dry; break me and change me into a holy vessel, worthy of Your service. Teach me right now what it means to be broken before You—before I fall under my own weight. I would rather be broken by You than be whole in the world. Thank You, Lord, that You are the Master Architect, and You see me now as I am supposed to be. Reshape me in Your image, Lord—use me as You see fit. I love You, and I trust You completely....

The Steps of a Man

"*From* ADONAI are *the steps of a man,*
And man—how [can] he understand his
way?" מִשְׁלֵי *Mish'lei (Proverbs) 20:24*

How is a child conceived in his mother's womb? Who gives a man his infant son to hold in his arms? In what manner does a child learn to speak and crawl and walk? By what power will he grow and someday have a son of his own?

One look into a newborn baby's face and we see the awesome power of God, yet we have no understanding of it. By His will—by a single thought in His mind— two microscopic cells become one, then two again, miraculously growing into a thinking, responding, seeing, hearing life form. Who can understand it? Who can fathom it? ADONAI forms each child in His own image—the Creator makes tiny beings that look just like Him.

As new creations in Messiah, so the hand of the Creator also forms us. Who can explain why one moment we are in sin, and the next we know our salvation? What takes place that causes us to be born again from above? How is the formerly hidden suddenly revealed, and we see clearly that to which we were formerly blind? By what power do we grow and someday have spiritual sons and daughters of our own?

In Messiah, our ways are God's ways, yet who can understand the ways of God? Though we do not understand, we *believe*. With our own eyes, we see the working of ADONAI in our lives. As we pursue wisdom, insight, balance, knowledge, and discipline, we are enabled to follow the pattern set out before us and walk in His divinely ordered steps. And in the Messiah Yeshua, we have the One who has trodden the way before us—who laid out a clearly marked path to follow, and did not stray to the left or right.

From ADONAI are the steps of a man, so we have security, protection, guidance, and unfailing provision. As we abide in Him, He resides in us—and understanding our own ways is no longer a prerequisite to obedience. Let us purpose in our hearts to follow the steps of the Master, forsaking our own way and abandoning our hearts to our God....

ॐ ᵕ

Father, Creator, You who perform miracles—I bless Your mighty Name! I praise You for Your awesomeness, Your unfathomable mysteries—You are beyond my understanding. ADONAI, I lean not on my own abilities, but trust You completely to guide my steps, to do miracles on my behalf, to make my roads straight and to remove obstacles in my path. Loving Father, I thank You for being above my comprehension, so that I will always rely only on You, my Source, my Rock, my Salvation....

More Than a Conqueror!

"Who will separate us from the love of the Messiah? Tribulation, or distress, or persecution, or famine, or nakedness, or peril, or sword? (according to what has been written—'For Your sake we are put to death all the day long; we were reckoned as sheep of slaughter.') But in all these we [are] more than [a] conqueror, through Him who loved us; for I am persuaded that neither death, nor life, nor messengers, nor principalities, nor powers, nor things present, nor things about to be, nor height, nor depth, nor any other created thing, shall be able to separate us from the love of God, that is in Messiah Yeshua our Master."
Romans 8:35-39

If only we could get this truth through our heads and hold it in our hearts: *nothing* will ever separate us from the love of the Messiah!

What is your biggest fear? Call it by name—stare it straight in the face. Through the love of Messiah, you are saved from death and given abundant life; you have authority over forces warring in the heavenlies and power over demons from hell. In Him, you are not bound by your past, trapped in your present, or hopeless for the future. There is no need to fear man, or any other thing in all creation. You are a not just a conqueror—but *more* than a conqueror!!! How threatening does that fear look now?

The love of God, from which we can *never* be separated, does not make us mere conquerors—it makes us *more than* conquerors. Our conquests surpass human reason, logic, and natural limits because our God goes before us, and He is above all our enemies! Not only are our foes vanquished and annihilated, but our losses are restored to us—and more than that, restored to us 30-, 60-, 100-fold! Because we are *more than* conquerors, we don't limp from the battlefield—we glide into glory.

If God is for us, who can be against us? Conventional wisdom—God confounds it. Public opinion—God ignores it. Is the Spirit of God telling you one thing while the people around you are saying another? Who will you believe? Can God act against the status quo? Can God circumvent the expected?

Believe the unbelievable: God is God. Be convinced: you are *more* than a conqueror—and there is absolutely nothing that can separate you from the love of God that is in Messiah Yeshua, our Master.

છે રહ્

Abba, Father, keep reminding me that nothing can separate me from Your love. Let me be convinced that despite my present circumstances—or even *because* of them—I am not *just* a conqueror, but *more* than a conqueror! Teach me to expect supernatural victories in every single area of my life. I am *more* than a conqueror, and no created thing—nothing dead, alive, past, present, future, angelic, or demonic—has the power to be victorious over me. I praise You, ADONAI, for *nothing* can separate me from You…

From the Depth

"And it was, when she prayed more and more before ADONAI, that עֵלִי, Eliy watched her mouth, and חַנָּה, Chanah spoke to her heart. [Since] only her lips were moving but her voice was not heard, עֵלִי, Eliy thought her to be drunk. And עֵלִי, Eliy said to her, 'How long will you [stay] drunk? Turn aside your wine from yourself.' And חַנָּה, Chanah answered and said, 'No, my lord, a woman sharply pained in spirit I am, but wine and strong drink I have not drunk. Instead I pour out my soul before ADONAI. Think not [of] your handmaid as a daughter of worthlessness, for from the depth of my troubles and grief have I been speaking.'"
שְׁמוּאֵל א *Sh'muel Alef (1Samuel) 1:12-16*

Chanah's greatest anguish was being barren and childless… unfruitful. But as a result of a period of intense prayer, ADONAI blessed her with Sh'muel, whom she in turn gave to ADONAI for life-service as a *cohen* (priest). After the blessing of Sh'muel, Chanah was far from unfruitful, for God opened her womb again—not once, but five more times.

Consider the nature of Chanah's praying. To an outsider like Eliy, she appeared intoxicated. But why would intense, soul-reaching prayer look so demeaning? Perhaps it was not that her actions appeared to be *immoral*, but simply that Eliy had never before seen such *unrestraint* in prayer—and in his entire frame of reference, drunkenness was its closest relative. Chanah was praying in such a way that she was able to reach God by speaking to her own heart—at the expense of appearing pious, restrained... or *normal.*

In times of anguish and distress, we tend to drown ourselves with extra-fleshly devices: food, drink, entertainment, drugs, sex, our jobs—and maybe even "the ministry." We allow ourselves to be consumed by things that do not *solve* our problems; they simply *mask* them... but only for a time. Look again at Chanah. Instead of pouring wine and liquor *down* her throat to deaden the effects of her depression, she turned to ADONAI and *poured out* the depths of her being to Him. Our answer is never to fill ourselves up with that which harms instead of heals—it is to *empty* ourselves before ADONAI, that He may restore our souls.

When we are depressed, anguished and distressed, it is then that we must *abandon* ourselves to ADONAI. To clear out what is inside, we must dig down to our deepest grief; and then, from the depth of our pain, we pour it out before ADONAI. We do not take into account our appearance—to others, and especially to ourselves—but we offer a prayer to ADONAI that He *will* remember....

ও⚬ ⚬৯

Father, teach me to abandon myself to You, to empty myself to You, to pour out my heart before You. Show me that no obstacle or hindrance in my limited wisdom is a true barrier to You—not how I look, how I act, what I say, or where I am.... Lord, may You alone be my source for peace and salvation. As I speak to You with my mouth, please hear the words from the depth of my innermost being...

He Has Never Seen

"*Because the wicked has boasted of the desire of his soul, And has blessed [those who] gain dishonestly, He has despised ADONAI. The wicked, like [someone with] his nose [held] high, [does] not seek after [God]. 'God is not!' are all his devices... He has said in his heart, 'I am not moved, [From] generation [to] generation [I will] not [suffer] in evil....' The wicked says in his heart, 'God has forgotten, He has hidden His face, He has never seen.'*" תְּהִלִּם *T'hillim (Psalms) 10:3-4, 6, 11*

The mark of the wicked is total depravity—not just depravity in action, but in *mind*. Our thoughts precede our actions—that's what makes sin so insidious. We have to agree with temptation, partner with the enemy, and declare allegiance to our flesh before proceeding with a sinful act.

To be depraved is to live in a veiled, clouded state—to encounter the world around us through the physical senses, yet to act as if things appear differently than they really are: to hear a curse, and call it a blessing; to smell a stench, and call it sweet; to taste a poison, and call it food; to see an innocent person, and lustfully fantasize; to touch what belongs to someone else, and call it one's own.

With a depraved mind, we see everything through the filter of our own flesh, our own desires and wants. Controlled by our arrogance, we run amuck—we move beyond abandon into pure self-indulgence, saying, *"God is not!... I am not moved... God has forgotten, He has hidden His face, He has never seen."* Here is the key to releasing the sinner from captivity to his own flesh: the shock of shame that comes upon him when he finally realizes that God *has* been watching—and waiting—all along.... waiting, to show him mercy and grace, to love him, and separate him from his sin.

Our part in bringing the sinner into the light of Messiah is to cut through the underbrush of lies and false reality, marking a clear path to ADONAI with the testimony of our faith and the Word of God. This is why we immerse ourselves in the Scriptures and spend time alone with God—so that we will be saturated with the light of life and have enough power to slice the thickest darkness in two. Only by staying pure and holy ourselves will the light of Messiah not be diminished through us, and we can be a beacon which leads the sinner to true life.

Father, cleanse me of my sins; blot out the memory of my transgressions. Let me be pure and spotless, so that I will not cast shadows of falsehood, but shine only Your holy light. Lift the veil of deception, clear the cloud of confusion that surrounds me, and let me stand before You—naked and unashamed. Change me and make me righteous once and for all, that I may see the truth of knowing You. I praise You, ADONAI, for showing me Your light... and for leaving it burning until I finally came home....

A Fool's Eyes Wander

"The face of the understanding [person] is toward wisdom, And the eyes of a fool—[they wander] to the end of the earth." מִשְׁלֵי *Mish'lei (Proverbs) 17:24*

Our natural tendency is to forego the plain things under our nose for romantic notions of the future. If we are not careful, we allow our desire for greener pastures to cause us to lose interest in the common things of our everyday lives, reducing their value in exchange for what will eventually be tomorrow's leftovers—and the cycle continues.

"The face of the understanding [person] is toward wisdom…" Often, the wisdom before us is not the most exciting thing in the world. Indeed, wisdom is quite plain and ordinary, in the sense that it governs our everyday lives. Day to day living in Messiah is not so much of an adventure, as it is a continual process of being transformed to holiness and godliness. Practically speaking, we need wisdom so that we can make the right choices in common, everyday situations. It is the understanding person who focuses on these things.

And yet, *"…the eyes of a fool—[they wander]…"* We need to realize that we are not called to be looking *"to the end of the earth"* in order to find the next mountain to climb or ocean to cross. Invariably, the one who is always looking for the next adventure will never be satisfied—and wisdom will fail to take root. We are naturally self-destructive in our tendencies to lose interest in those things that we formerly believed to be important—we cast them aside for what seems like a more exciting alternative. Eventually, we lose interest again, and continue in the unhealthy pattern where nothing is able to satisfy.

Wisdom requires deep roots. The person with understanding does not simply change his mind because the thrill is gone. One who is wise will wait through the honeymoon, knowing that the truly fulfilling things lie ahead. If we get up and go as soon as the romance wears off, we will never be able to exercise the wisdom of Messiah in our lives. We will continue to wander aimlessly, always looking for the next, more challenging mountain. Our destiny lies in our ability to be fulfilled as we wait…

❧ ❧

ADONAI, I wait upon You. Show me the wisdom that is before me, and teach me to focus completely upon it. Lord, keep me from foolish ways; cause my eyes to no longer wander. Help me to focus on the task before me, that I will participate fully in the completion of what You have begun. You are worthy of praise, my Father, for You are a patient God. Teach me Your ways, that I may be a person of understanding…

God Doesn't Do Monthlies

"*[Yeshua said,] 'Two debtors were to a certain creditor… one owing five hundred day's wages, and the other fifty, and [neither] having the wherewithal to give back, the creditor forgave both. Which, then, of them, do you say, will love the creditor more?' And שִׁמְעוֹן, Shim'on answered, 'I suppose that to whom the creditor forgave the more;' and Yeshua said to him, 'Rightly you did judge.'*" Luke 7:41-43

For some of us, it's hard to remember that mercy triumphs over justice. We have it drilled into our heads that sin is sin is sin. We think, steal a penny, steal a dollar—it's all the same to God, and it's all counted alike. That's pretty self-condemning. Thank God that, in the end, we do not sit in judgment of ourselves— many of us would pass sentence without even hearing the case! This self-loathing also translates into a judgmental relationship with others, believers and unbelievers alike. We must remember what brought us to ADONAI in the first place: it was not our sin—it was His *forgiveness* of our sin. In our minds, however, we sometimes get it backwards.

Yeshua paints a picture of perfect release. To our minds, all sin is equal; but to the mind of God, not all *forgiveness* is equal. Where more forgiveness is required, more is given, and how much greater the gift becomes. Sin is still sin, but God is still God. He is in the business of forgiving sin—all sin, of all shapes and sizes—and He has custom-made forgiveness to fit our need.

This should give us incredible hope! No matter how far we have crawled from Him, our Abba Father is capable—and best of all, willing—to offer his forgiveness. If we are steeped in sin, He can forgive. If we are backslidden to the point that we are unable to get back up, He can forgive. Even if we have simply forgotten how to come into His presence daily and make him the master of our life, He can forgive.

When we buy on credit with sin, ADONAI can cancel—clean up—our debt. But He doesn't just pay the monthly minimum due… no, the burden of debt to oppression and the grave is erased altogether! We are released and set free by the forgiveness of sins through the atoning sacrifice of Messiah Yeshua. Truly, we are unable to reimburse The Creditor. Just think about how big your debt has been, and be filled with gratefulness, thanksgiving and love that it is no longer counted against you.

ॐ ॐ

Master Yeshua, by the shedding of Your innocent blood, You have paid the debt I bought with sin. Thank You for Your love! I see the extent of Your forgiveness —it is overflowing! Truly, I am unable to save myself… but You are Yeshua, You are Salvation, and You have saved me from my sin. Thank You, Master, for washing me clean, canceling the debt, and giving me a fresh start. In You, I am renewed every morning, and I devote my life—everything I say and do—to You…

There Is a Choice

"… for the pain accomplished by God [brings] repentance to salvation—it does not bring regret—but the pain of the world brings death." 2Corinthians 7:10

The Word of God promises pain. It is inevitable; unavoidable… it's part of life. No one can avert pain. Consider Paul—who can compare? Consider the Master Himself—who experienced greater pain than He? Believe it: we *will* be afflicted. However, from all afflictions and pain, we can be set free!

When we experience pain, what do we do? We complain, bellyache, moan and groan. We cry and weep, and throw ourselves on our own anguish. We grieve and become ill, sickening ourselves with our distress. We slowly and surely wither away, twinge and spasm, spiraling and sinking into the pit. Our minds and bodies weaken, becoming brittle and frail. Our spirits and souls are parched, arid and abandoned. The world's way of handling pain isn't handling it at all— the world's way is to embrace it, to love it, to be enamored with it, to suckle on it. Death becomes the lover of a dying soul.

"The pain accomplished by God," on the other hand, is just the opposite. Indeed, *you* don't have to handle it at all! Your pain needs to drag itself to the foot of the Tree, be hoisted upon the shoulders of Messiah and crucified… *once and for all.* Then bow down there and watch your Savior bleed; see Him die under the weight

of your pain on His back. Watch them bury him in a tomb. Then be amazed, astounded, enthralled and overjoyed, as God raises Him from the dead with your pain nowhere to be found....

When we allow God to handle our pain, it produces repentance—a turning from sin to God. Repentance then leads to salvation—being saved from our oppression, depression, affliction, suffering, hardship, persecution, pain... and, yes, even death. The pain of the world brings only death, but the pain accomplished by God brings salvation—*"it does not bring regret."*

So whose pain will be accomplished in your life? Turn from sin, turn to God, abandon your pain, and die today for the very last time—die to yourself and gain Messiah... and, finally, once and for all, live!

જે ન્હ્ર

Lord Yeshua, I receive the freedom Your sacrifice brings. I now and forever turn away from my sin—in the midst of my filth and stench, I turn to You and accept Your love that makes me clean. I don't want to die—I want to live! I don't want pain—I want life and freedom! Thank You, God, that I don't need to even touch my pain, but that You will take care of it for me. I love You, Father, and I give myself completely and totally to You with no regrets. I receive Your love and Your salvation... Your Son...

A Better King

"*And the thing was evil in the eyes of* שְׁמוּאֵל, *Sh'muel, when they said, 'Give to us a king to judge us;' and* שְׁמוּאֵל, *Sh'muel prayed to* ADONAI. *And* ADONAI *said to* שְׁמוּאֵל, *Sh'muel, 'Listen to the voice of the people, to all that they say to you, for you they have not rejected, but Me they have rejected, from reigning over them. According to all the works that they have done from the day of My bringing them up out of Egypt, even to this day, when they forsake Me, and serve other gods —so they are doing also to you....' And the people refused to listen to the voice of* שְׁמוּאֵל, *Sh'muel, and said, 'No, but a king we want over us, and we will be, even we, like all the nations; and our king will judge us, and go out before us, and fight our battles.'"* שְׁמוּאֵל א *Sh'muel Alef (1Samuel) 8:6-8; 19-20*

The scheme of the evil one is to take a good idea and skew it *just enough* so that it will take us light-years off course. Yis'rael understood that she needed a king —a moral center, a leader, a protector. But instead of looking to ADONAI, she was enticed to be *"like all the nations."* Yis'rael could not accept that she was to be *unlike* the nations—that her model for morality, leadership and protection was not of the world, but of the kingdom of God.

ADONAI explains the peoples' motives, saying, *"Me they have rejected, from reigning over them"*—yet, they still wanted a king. How is it that the kingship of ADONAI was insufficient for them? Yis'rael fell into the trap of "out of sight, out of mind," believing their lying eyes rather than trusting the reality of God. The nation needed a king, but the good idea was perverted. Instead of an "invisible" God, they wanted a man of flesh and blood.

How often do we set up man against God? What does it say about us when we look for solutions in the limited wisdom of man rather than the unfathomable knowledge of our God? When we don't see God with our eyes, when we can't reach out and touch him with our hands, our trust wanes and we turn to that which we believe we can trust above all else—our own senses.

There is no king but the King of Kings, yet the One who alone deserves kingship is the One most often rejected. ADONAI wants to be king over us—*not* so that we can be like all the nations, but to set us apart from the world and empower us to be holy as He is holy. We rightly want our king to judge us, lead us and fight our battles—but only King Messiah, ADONAI himself, is ready, willing, and able.

Isn't it plain to *see*?

இ் ஊ்

ADONAI, King of my life—rule and reign, that I might be a loyal subject in Your kingdom. I need Your protection, Your guidance, Your holiness. In return, I submit to You completely… no earthly authority can compare. Father, thank You for being my King and for loving me enough to forgive me when I reject You over and over again. I praise You for Your patience; I worship You for Your faithfulness. You are always true to Your word—teach me to trust You more, my "invisible" King…

Your Own Mouth

"Let another [person] praise you, and not your own mouth—a stranger, not your own lips." מִשְׁלֵי *Mish'lei (Proverbs) 27:2*

As fragile human beings, we are always looking for approval or validation. Those of us with an over-developed ego seem to suffer from this the most—the higher our opinion of ourselves, the more we crave recognition. Regardless, it is often difficult for us to go through life without hearing praise from the people around us. Thus, we resort to drawing attention to ourselves through self-exaltation.

The scheme works—for a little while. As our mouth declares our praises, people take notice and listen. But slowly, they begin to realize that *we* are speaking these wonderful things about *ourselves*. It doesn't take long for them to notice that we fall short of how wonderful we claim to be, and their admiration turns to contempt.

Now, when another *person* praises us—that's a different story. Not only do people take notice of us, but they *believe* the report is *true*. Their perception of us is affected, and we become truly praiseworthy in their eyes.

And even more, the validity of the report is increased exponentially when the praise comes from someone who *barely knows us at all*. When a friend or a family member sings our praises, it can be perceived as merely kind words from someone with a biased opinion. But when a *stranger* praises us, his words are accepted as true, for it is clear that our *reputation* has gone before us.

"*Let another [person] praise you, and not your own mouth—a stranger, not your own lips.*" Our praises will be on the lips of strangers because of how we serve the people who know us. When we praise ourselves, who can testify about our character? But when others hold us in high esteem, their voices give witness to our inner qualities of praiseworthiness, and our path will be made smooth before us.

Believe this: you are worthy of praise already if you are in right standing with God—now go and serve with diligence and humility… and soon, strangers will give you praise!

       ও আ

Abba, Father, I bless Your name, and I give *You* all of my praise. Let me never sing my own praises, but make me a humble servant who follows only Your ways. If I am praised, Lord, may it be because You live through me and I in You. You alone are worthy of praise, and Your praise is the only one that I seek. You are awesome, Mighty God—thank You for allowing me to serve….

Trading Insult
for Blessing

"Blessed are you when men hate you, and when they separate you [from themselves], and insult [you], and cast forth your name as evil for [the] sake of the Son of Man—rejoice in that day, and leap [for joy], for behold, your reward is great in the Heaven. For according to these things were their fathers doing [the same] to the prophets." Luke 6:22-23

As disciples of Messiah, how often do we leap for joy when things are going well, much less when we stand in the face of adversity? It's strange and hard to believe that persecution is reason for gladness; and, indeed, it is not —unless the cause is for the Master. Sometimes, however, it is not our *cause* that leads to persecution—instead, in our flesh, we bring it upon ourselves.

A believer with a lofty view of "lowly sinners" can himself be the cause and the source of the complaints against him. Yeshua is offensive enough—He doesn't need our help. The Good News offends sin. It stirs sin's hatred. As we seek holiness and purity before ADONAI, the radiance of our flesh fades, and the light of Yeshua shines through. Light offends darkness, infiltrating and exposing the hidden things.

When we encounter people who hate, ostracize, insult and denounce us, on whose account is it? Have we taken the log from our own eye before dealing with the splinter in another's? We will be blessed if the insults we receive are on account of Yeshua; but if it is on our own account, we will not be blessed—we will merely be insulted.

Never seek to offend, and you will still be offensive. Never seek to confront, and you will be confronted. Don't hide the light and love of Yeshua, but boldly let it shine! As we remove ourselves, the darkness will be penetrated, and it will lash out in our direction. Rejoice, be blessed, because it is not you that is being attacked, but the Master *in* you. The reward that awaits us is not for the offenses we cause with our own words and actions, but for the light of the Good News that agitates, disturbs, and disrupts the slumber of the world.

Rejoice when you are hated; yes, leap for joy! If you stand before ADONAI in innocence, the world will pronounce you guilty—and this is reason for joy… because now is the time to shine.

≈ ∾

ADONAI, only You know the hearts of all men—only You can judge and pass sentence. Teach me daily to step aside, that You may rise up and be magnified. Father, give me clean hands and a pure heart, that I may be innocent as I stand before You. Give me Your boldness and strength, that I may be a witness—a living testimony of Your greatness. As I speak, let it be You speaking through me, so that all they will see is You….

*"Greet Epaenetus, my beloved [friend],
who is the first-fruits in Asia to [accept]
Messiah." Romans 16:5b*

Epaenetus—perhaps the greatest, most widely known
and influential believer of first century Asia. Even today,
we study his life in elaborate detail. Generations have
been impacted beyond measure, with scores of volumes
dedicated to the effects of his ministry...

Who?

Indeed, who—all facetiousness aside—was Epaenetus?
All that was *truly* recorded of this believer is a footnote
in Paul's closing remarks in a letter to the Messianic
believers in Rome. Yet, God, who breathed all of Paul's
writings to life, chose little, insignificant Epaenetus to
leave his footprints—as small as they might be—on the
sands of Scripture. Why? Certainly, Epaenetus was
distinguished with the honor of being the first person
in Asia to receive Yeshua. That's definitely newsworthy
information. But the beauty is that there is nothing
unique about Epaenetus at all—he was merely given
the distinct honor of being the first.

How often do we sit around feeling sorry for ourselves that we haven't accomplished enough for God?
How often do we feel like giving up, that we haven't
made an impact on anyone's life—in fact, we're barely
keeping our own head above water.... What good are
we, anyway? Now is a good time to take another look at

Epaenetus. What did *he* do that was so great? If he had done something truly noteworthy, Paul would have certainly brought it up, right? Epaenetus isn't really so great....

On the contrary, God has made Epaenetus famous. This footnote in the history of our faith has been glorified for eternity in the strokes and letters of the Scriptures of God! What wouldn't you do, what wouldn't you give, for God to glorify *you* like that—to be so pleased with you and your life that He would honor you with such distinction? And still, what do we know that Epaenetus really did? Truth be told: nothing... Except he *accepted* Messiah.

We have to start somewhere with ADONAI. Sometimes, we even have to start over! But no matter where we are in our walk with Him, it always comes back to basics. Sure, we want God to be pleased with us—to glorify us for His Name's sake. But when all is said and done, what truly makes the difference is simply that we *accepted* Messiah.

֍ ֍

Father, make Yourself famous in my life. Hal'lu Yah, I boast in You! Thank You for loving me before I was ever loving; thank You for being pleased with me before I was ever pleasing; thank You for putting Your trust in me before I was ever trusting. Let me grow smaller in my own eyes every day, as You make Yourself greater in my walk with You. Remind me that even though You want me to grow up, I'm still Your little child, and You're still pleased with me, Mighty God....

Go Out and Stand

"And אֵלִיָּהוּ, *Eliyahu came in there, to the cave, and
lodged there, and behold, the word of* ADONAI *came to him,
and said to him, 'What are you [doing] here,* אֵלִיָּהוּ, *Eliyahu?' And he answered, 'I have been very zealous for* ADONAI
…*Your prophets, they have been slain by the sword, and I
am left, I, by myself, and they seek my life—to take it.' And*
ADONAI *said, 'Go out, and stand on the mountain before*
ADONAI.' *And behold,* ADONAI *passed by, and a wind—
great and strong—rent [the] mountains, and rocks shivered
before* ADONAI: *—[but] not in the wind was* ADONAI; *and
after the wind [came] a shaking:—[but] not in the shaking
was* ADONAI; *and after the shaking [came] a fire:—[but] not
in the fire was* ADONAI; *and after the fire [came] a voice still
[and] small; and it came to pass, at* אֵלִיָּהוּ, *Eliyahu hearing
it, that he wrapped his face in his robe, and went out, and
stood at the opening of the cave, and behold, to him came a
voice, and it said, 'What are you [doing] here,* אֵלִיָּהוּ, *Eliyahu?' And he answered, 'I have been very zealous for* ADONAI
…*Your prophets, they have been slain by the sword, and I
am left, I, by myself, and they seek my life—to take it.'"*
מְלָכִים א *M'lachiym Alef (1Kings) 19:9-14*

"What are you [doing] here?" He asks us. "Why are
you hiding? From what are you running?" We answer,
cowering in our dark cave, "Don't you know what's
going on in my life? In the past, I have been zealous for
You, ADONAI, but now I am all alone and there is no
one to protect me. I am vulnerable, I am exposed—
my destruction surely awaits me."

ADONAI answered Eliyahu's fears. "You're afraid, are you, Eliyahu? I'll show you something to be afraid of..." "*A wind—great and strong—rent [the] mountains.*" Eliyahu stood his ground; ADONAI was not in the wind. "*After the wind*" came an earthquake. Eliyahu was not shaken; ADONAI was not in the earthquake. "*After the shaking [came] a fire.*" Eliyahu remained unsinged; ADONAI was not in the fire. "*And after the fire [came] a voice still [and] small.*" Eliyahu covered his face—this was the voice of God.

It is not the troubles of life that we should fear, but the One who can *save* us from them with only a word from His mouth. He is in complete control of everything, and He will never harm us or leave us. Instead, He will protect us from our enemies and save us from death. Eliyahu finally understood this and stepped out of his cave to stand on the mountain of God.

ADONAI asks again, "*What are you [doing] here?*" And we answer in exactly the same way as before. "In the past, I have been zealous for you, ADONAI, but I am all alone and there is no one to protect me from my enemies. *No one, that is, but you, ADONAI, and that is all I need to know.*"

&ণ্ড ক্ত

My Protector, my Deliverer, I worship and praise You with all my being, for You are all-powerful, all-knowing, ever-present, never-failing. I fear You, Creator, with a holy fear; yet I come close to You in reverence, knowing that I can rest my head on You and fall into Your arms. Thank You, Father, for Your still, small voice that is so awesome and great in the earth! Teach me to hear Your voice even in the worst of circumstances. ADONAI, I abandon myself—my whole life—to You...

What Is Right?

"To do your pleasure, my God, I have delighted, And your תּוֹרָה, *Torah is within my heart. I have proclaimed [the] good news of righteousness In the great assembly, behold, my lips I restrain not, O ADONAI, You have known. Your righteousness I have not concealed In the midst of my heart, Your faithfulness and Your salvation I have told, I have not hidden Your kindness and Your truth, To the great assembly."* תְּהִלִּם *T'hillim (Psalms) 40:8-10*

One of the most difficult things for us as disciples of Messiah is to boldly proclaim the *"good news of righteousness."* Perhaps this is not because we are adverse to the act of proclaiming, but because we don't actually know *"the good news of righteousness."* Instead of announcing His truth, we just end up spreading our own *opinions*.

To our minds, "truth" is relative—an elusive concept formulated from our own experiences. Even ideas that are biblically based often diverge into what we individually consider "truth." Because of this, it is difficult to find any agreement within the Body of Messiah. We interpret God's Truth through our own filters of experience, and inevitably find ourselves at a distance from other believers.

David says that he *"proclaimed [the] good news of righteousness."* Who is David, a mere mortal, that he so clearly knows what is right? He claims that he did not conceal God's kindness and truth. But how does David know that what he revealed was certainly the truth and kindness of God? The key to David's life is that in his inmost being, he delighted in doing ADONAI's pleasure —and God's Word was within his heart.

The Word of God is absolute—it is our sole source of authoritative Truth. Anything outside, underneath, on top of, or beside the Scriptures is not Truth. Every book on our shelves, every word written by men of renown… and, most of all, this little devotional—they're just people's ideas. We need to ask ourselves the hard question: are we willing to obey the Word of God without first sifting it through our experiential opinions? Will we delight only in His pleasure, hiding not His kindness and truth?

ॐ ॐ

Abba, Father, may my lips not be restrained, but may I boldly declare Your faithfulness and salvation! Your grace and truth have been covered over by my own traditions and opinions—forgive me! Abba, make me a child that responds to You, rather than to the past situations of my life. ADONAI, it is my joy to do Your will—help me to set apart Your Voice from the noise of experience. Guide me in Your truth, and teach me….

God Doesn't Speak to Me Like That

"And it came to pass, [while] all the people [were] being immersed, Yeshua also [was] being immersed and praying, [when] the heaven was opened, and the רוּחַ הַקֹּדֶשׁ, *Ruach HaKodesh* came down in a bodily form, as if a dove, upon him, and a voice came out of heaven, saying, 'You are My Son—the Beloved, in you I [do] delight.'" *Luke 3:21-22*

We've all pleaded with ADONAI from time to time for a sign that we're doing all right—a descending dove, even an audible voice from heaven would be nice.... We figure, there *must* be something that we can start doing —or stop doing—that will result in clear direction for our lives. We hope for assurance that despite what we see with our physical eyes, our situation will improve or take a miraculous turn for the better. Oh, if only we could put our finger on what it is God wants us to do....

"I love you, son. I am quite delighted with you." Every child longs to hear the encouragement of a father. But at the time Yeshua heard these words from *His* Father, what had He done to warrant such praise? Maybe he had performed many miracles, releasing the oppressed from their captivity. Perhaps He had even been persecuted by His enemies. Surely, He must have

exhibited great faith by boldly proclaiming the Good
News.

But when the Father spoke these words of approval
to His Son, He had not done *any* of these things. The
great things Yeshua was to accomplish for the kingdom
were yet to come. All He was doing when He heard the
praises of God was *"being immersed and praying."*

To be immersed, covered, submerged, surrounded,
embraced by ADONAI—deep in His presence, in worship
and praise, drowning in His Word, giving thanks for
His greatness and glory for His faithfulness… And in
prayer—to be one with the Father, having fellowship in
the Spirit, being washed clean again, listening for His
still and quiet voice, and hearing Him more clearly and
distinctly each time….

In our minds, we think that if we could just get a
definite response from the Lord, this would be all the
encouragement, reassurance, and empowerment we
would need. But it is our devotion and dedication to
ADONAI—our pure love for Him—that will cause us to
hear the loving voice of God. As we immerse ourselves
in Him, He will immerse us in Himself. What we are
going to do for ADONAI will come later—first, we just
need to be immersed in Him, and be embraced by His
love… all over again.

ॐ ॐ

Father, ADONAI, immerse me in Your *Ruach
HaKodesh.* I desire nothing more than to be in Your
presence, completely surrounded by Your love. Thank
You for loving me first, for showing Yourself faithful in
my life. I give You glory for the mighty things You have
done! Receive my worship and praise, and draw me
closer to You. Wrap me in Your arms, Abba, and let me
tell You how much I love You….

Run to Win!

"Have you not known that those running in a race—all indeed run, but [only] one wins the prize? So run, that you will win! Every athletic contestant is in all things disciplined; these, indeed, then, may win a corruptible [laurel] wreath, but we an incorruptible [one]. I, therefore, run, not as uncertainly; I fight, as not [just] beating air; but I beat my body [black and blue], and bring it into servitude, lest by any means, having preached to others—I myself may become disqualified." 1Corinthians 9:24-27

I'm tired of running the race... always running, running... Can't we stop for water? Just let me catch my breath. I think I need to take a week off—make that two. What's that? Lord, I'm completely wiped out— I really need some time off. Can't You just leave me *alone* for once? Listen, I'm just going to stop here for a while. I'll catch up with You later... No, really, You go on without me...

What motivated Paul to run the race? Was it Love? Passion? Fear? Obedience? Adrenaline rush? Spiritual fulfillment? Perhaps it was a little of all these things. But Paul preached the Good News for one reason and one reason only: God said. What God said, Paul did. No other reason was required.

But, surely, Paul must have had some special anointing to run such a straight race—always staying on track, never wandering aimlessly, never getting distracted with "beating air," and persevering on the course despite its obstacles. What did Paul have that made him so effective?

Simple... Discipline.

Well, simple, yes. Easy, no.

Paul was successful at self-discipline because he understood the importance of *submission*. We know in our minds that discipline is the key to perseverance, yet we allow our flesh to dictate our tolerance level. If we submit to ADONAI's discipline—rather than what we *think* we're capable of enduring—it teaches us our true potential. Our legs get steadier, our heart pumps stronger, the path gets straighter, the mountains seem lower and the valleys higher. If we refuse to submit to discipline, the race makes *us*—but with *God's* discipline, *we* make the race. So then, run to win....

కా oయ

ADONAI, teach me Your discipline. Correct me, rebuke me, encourage me, affirm me—as You will, Father, I receive it. Teach me how to disregard my fleshly complaints and listen only to the discipline of the Spirit. Teach me submission to Your discipline, that I may persevere, run a good and straight race, and win. Let me leave my flesh in the dust as I kick up my heels and head toward the finish line. For Your glory, Father, I submit....

God Who?

> "And the messenger of ADONAI came and sat
> under the pistachio tree... and the messenger of
> ADONAI appeared to גִּדְעוֹן, Gid'on, and said to
> him, 'ADONAI is with you, O mighty one of valor.'
> And גִּדְעוֹן, Gid'on said to him, 'Excuse me, sir—
> but [if] ADONAI is with us!—then why has all
> this [trouble] found us? And where are all his won-
> ders which our fathers recounted to us, saying,
> "Has not ADONAI brought us up out of Egypt?"
> And now ADONAI has left us, and gives us into
> the hands of מִדְיָן, Mid'yan.'" שֹׁפְטִים Shof'tiym
> (Judges) 6:11-13

How many times have we cried out in our anguish,
"[If] ADONAI is with us, then why has all this [trouble]
found us?" God is nowhere to be seen, so we conclude,
"ADONAI has left us..." But just because we have been
"found" by trouble, this is not grounds to believe that
God is gone.

ADONAI first appears to Gid'on in an apparently
unconvincing manner, sitting under the pistachio tree.
How often does ADONAI sit and wait patiently for us to
recognize Him? Indeed, our natural response to Him is
often the same as Gid'on's. He calls us "mighty one of
valor" and proclaims His presence to us, yet what is our
response? "Excuse me sir—but..."

Why did Gid'on interrogate ADONAI in this manner?
Was it because he didn't believe he was in the presence

of God? Was he simply ignorant? Was he being careful to determine he was not being fooled?

After Yis'rael's forty years of peace and her decline away from the presence of ADONAI, Gid'on didn't really give God's promises to Yis'rael any thought at all. In fact, the salvation of ADONAI was so far from Gid'on's mind that even the appearance of ADONAI Himself was not enough to stir him. All he had was a fading memory of what he had been *told* God had done and would do for Yis'rael. Gid'on's personal experience with God was so diminished that he couldn't recognize ADONAI even when He appeared under a pistachio tree!

We ask the Lord, "Where are you?"—not because He has left us, but because we have forgotten what He looks like and where to seek Him. We ask the Lord, "Where are your wonders?"—not because we notice they are missing, but because ADONAI prompts us, blind as we are, by showing Himself to us.

Truly, He is never far from us—even when we ask His whereabouts in the midst of His presence. Indeed, we will know that we are abandoned only when we stop wondering where He is.

෨ ෧

ADONAI, let me never fall so far from You that I cannot hear Your voice or recognize Your face. Teach me to never doubt Your provision and Your promises, but to always expect You—even when I don't see You. Let me always be pleasantly surprised by Your appearance —may it never become commonplace or foreign, but continually astonishing. ADONAI, I love to be near to You. Never let Yourself become a distant memory to me, but be a perpetual presence *in* me every moment of my life....

Reproof to the Wise

*"The corrector of a scorner receives for it—
shame, And a reprover of the wicked—his
blemish. Do not reprove a scorner, lest he will
hate you; Give reproof to the wise, and he will
love you."* מִשְׁלֵי *Mish'lei (Proverbs) 9:7-8*

According to the Scriptures, there are times when
we must correct and reprove one another for the edifica-
tion of both the individual and the greater community.
While we do not seek out occasions to correct—nor is it
something that we necessarily enjoy— reproof and
correction are important for us as disciples of Messiah.
However, this principle doesn't apply to everyone—it
only works within the context of a properly functioning
relationship with another *believer*.

The scorner and the wicked man reject God and His
ways—by definition, they reject the standard of Scripture.
The scorner will shame you and the wicked man will
become your blemish because you have no right or
privilege to give them correction. Between you and the
person who rejects ADONAI, there is no standard upon
which a reproof can be based. You cannot speak correction into the life of an unbeliever and expect fruitful
results.

True relationship cannot exist between two people
unless Yeshua is their common bond—a believer and an
unbeliever simply have no basis to make a proper connection. There may be commonalities and mutual associa-
tions, but a true relationship is one in which each person

can respond to the other with the love of Yeshua—
especially when one is giving and the other is receiving
correction. /

Yet even among believers, correction does not
always result in an outpouring of love. Indeed, we often
receive *"shame"* and a *"blemish"* for our efforts. While
being on the receiving end of a rebuke isn't pleasant, we
must make a choice as to how we will respond. Will we
be like the scorner who has only hatred for the one
bringing correction, or will we answer with the love of
our Master? Enduring reproof with hostility benefits no
one—but the one who receives correction in love is
wise.

ॐ ॐ

ADONAI, send Your correction and reproof into my
life, though I have been hurt by people who have abused
it before. Abba, Father, place me in a healthy, safe, community of like-minded believers—even in times of
loneliness, preserve me for a group of people who will
show me love and whom I may love in return. Teach
me to give and receive reproof in love and wisdom, that
I may grow and abound in You. I praise You, Father, for
leading me into relationships that are founded upon
You alone, and will bring glory to Your name...

Soil for the Seed

"And this is the parable: The seed is the word of God. And those beside the path are those hearing; then the Adversary comes, and takes up the word from their heart, lest having believed, they may be saved. And those upon the rock: They who, when they hear, receive the word with joy. But these, who for a time believe, have no root, and in time of temptation fall away. And that which fell to the thorns: These are they who have heard, and going forth, through anxieties, and riches, and pleasures of life, are choked, and bear not to completion. And that in the good ground: These are they, who in an upright and good heart, having heard the word, retain it, and bear fruit continually." Luke 8:11-15

Path: trodden, untilled soil. Such ground cannot be penetrated, and the seeds are easily plucked away. We need to be broken up, the tough surface crushed, and our rich soil exposed, so that we can be receptive to the planting of God's Word in our heart. This isn't easy, and it may take some time. But as we make ourselves open and vulnerable, we find that God does not leave us exposed. Instead, He carefully places His Word inside us, waters it with the showers of the *Ruach HaKodesh*, and saves us with the atonement of the Lamb.

Rock: petrified matter. Just receiving the seed with joy does not mean that the plant will grow. No, joy's roots must grow deep if we are to have the strength of ADONAI. If our joy is only on the surface, we will soon be *petrified* by fear—it will obstruct our growth, and the temptations of life will cause us to fall away. Those deposits of fear need to be dissolved and replaced with The Deposit of the *Ruach HaKodesh*—our joy, comfort, and assurance in the face of all troubles.

Thorns: sharp, spiny protuberances. If we can't be stopped with fear, the Adversary tries a more subtle approach—he turns us on ourselves. The more we focus on our own worries and concerns, the less we can see of ADONAI. We end up suffocating ourselves with our own self-made pressures, needs and distractions. In the end, the little that does end up growing is not cared for or nurtured—it is withered, atrophied and useless.

Good ground: suitable for growth. Fertile soil that is prepared to receive a new implantation will yield much fruit and a harvest for the kingdom of God. As we hold on to the Word of God, we can withstand all attacks. Because he only sees what is on the surface, the Adversary doesn't understand why his best-laid plans continue to fail. But in the Spirit, we see *beneath* the surface, where our roots are stretching deep into the soil. Our foundation is strong; and we are able to withstand the tests, persevere, and produce much fruit.

ॐ ॐ

Lord, show me where I am in my walk with You; reveal to me the true condition of my heart. Renew and guide me, that I may be rich soil for Your Word. Make me good ground to receive a new implantation of You. I want to bring a harvest into the kingdom, that You alone may be glorified. Teach me to live a life fully devoted to You—free from unbrokenness, fear, and worry… that my roots may grow deep….

We Say, "Witnesses!"

"And יְהוֹשֻׁעַ, Y'hoshua said to the people, 'You
are not able to serve ADONAI, for a God most holy
is He; a zealous God is He; He does not bear with
your transgression and with your sins. When you
desert ADONAI and serve [the] gods of a foreigner,
then He will turn back and do evil to you, and
consume you, [even] after that He has done good
to you.' And the people said to יְהוֹשֻׁעַ, Y'hoshua,
'No, but we serve ADONAI.' And יְהוֹשֻׁעַ, Y'hoshua
said to the people, 'Witnesses you are against
yourselves, that you have chosen for yourselves
ADONAI to serve Him (and they say, "Witnesses!")
and, now, turn aside [from] the gods of the
foreigner which are in your midst, and incline
your heart to ADONAI, God of יִשְׂרָאֵל, Yis'rael.'
And the people said to יְהוֹשֻׁעַ, Y'hoshua, 'ADONAI
our God we serve, and to His voice we listen.'"
יְהוֹשֻׁעַ, Y'hoshua (Joshua) 24:19-24

Y'hoshua's word to Yis'rael is pretty serious. The
commitment Yis'rael made to ADONAI that day spelled
condemnation for those who did not keep it. How much
more today, when we pledge ourselves to Messiah and
do not keep our word. Will we, too, bear the consequences
of an empty promise? How often have we sung songs,
shared a corporate prayer and testified, "We will serve…"
"We are witnesses…" "We listen to His voice…"? Our
testimony becomes a witness *against* us, and we are
judged by our own mouths.

It is a matter of *devotion*: we will serve the one to whom we are devoted. Y'hoshua urged, *"turn aside [from] the gods of the foreigner... and incline your heart to ADONAI."* Have you ever felt like you really want to spend more time devoted to God, but you just can't seem to squeeze it out of the day? Our family, spouse, children, job, ministry, and various other pursuits take up so much of our time that sometimes we even forego our daily devotions to the Holy One. Who, then—or what—receives our devotion?

ADONAI wants to *multiply* us—to make us stronger, more efficient vessels of His Will. He is completely aware of our obstacles, but is asking us today, "For whom do you live?" "Who do you serve?" How can we listen to His voice if we never stop long enough to *hear* Him? Draw closer to God—with your intent, your time, and your priorities—and He will *redeem* everything you "give up." There is nothing more important, more crucial to life, than devotion to the Father. He is not "part of the mix," nor an ingredient in the kitchen of life. ADONAI is the be-all, and end-all of our existence, and he *deserves* our devotion.

やや

Father, convict me of my insincerity. Teach me how to make You my life's focus and to find all my strength, power, energy, ideas, productivity—my everything—only in You. Show Yourself faithful in my life, so that as I draw closer to You, You will draw closer to me. I "sacrifice" my time to You—not so that it will be redeemed, but because You are worth far more than my time and attention. Thank You, Lord.... You are so awesome and mighty and worthy of praise—and I'll prove it to You with my actions....

Eat, Drink and Enjoy

"*Behold that which I have seen:* It is *good and beautiful [for a person] to eat, and to drink, and to enjoy [the] good in all one's work at which he labors under the sun the number of the days of his life that God has given to him —for it is his portion.*" קֹהֶלֶת *Kohelet (Ecclesiastes) 5:18*

After extreme experimentation to find that which is valuable and meaningful, Kohelet ("the Preacher") settles for this—almost as if it is too easy an answer. He voices these words as a consolation to himself, even as he remains dissatisfied with the answers he is finding in his search for the meaning of life.

In a brief respite from his discourse on the futility of man's existence, Kohelet admits that good may result from "*all one's work at which he labors under the sun the number of the days of his life that God has given to him.*" In his concession, Kohelet teaches us this simple truth: we may find pleasure—simple pleasure—in the work of our hands. It is our allotted portion in life, given by God as a gift that we may enjoy.

"*Eat… drink… and enjoy*" in another context might be considered inappropriate. But Kohelet judges this to be *"good"* and *"beautiful,"* because the simple pleasures of life are from God. He goes on to say that the one who has the power to enjoy the riches of his life *"does not think about the [shortness of the] days of his life, for God answers [him] through the joy of his heart."* (vs. 20) In other words, life is worth living when we enjoy our allotted portion—when we are *thankful* for what we have.

My grandmother used to say, "as long as you're healthy and happy...." This is the good life—having the power (health) to enjoy (happiness) our allotted portion. For Kohelet, this is "saving grace" for a life that is otherwise useless. Yet the simplicity of this truth is easily lost in our busy, "meaningless" lives. Perhaps we would do well to survey the good things that ADONAI has given us today, and to feast upon the simple things instead. Surely, it is in these that a man may enjoy all the days of his life....

ॐ ॐ

Abba, Father, thank You for the simple things in life—for my family, my job, the clothes on my back, the food on my table... I bless You, Lord, for all the good You have given me. Teach me to enjoy the good that results from all my work under the sun, that I may relish in my allotted portion in health and happiness. I praise You, my King, for You have held back nothing, so that my joy may be full....

Until I Hear Your Voice

"Fear of ADONAI is a beginning of knowledge;
wisdom and discipline fools have despised!"
מִשְׁלֵי *Mish'lei (Proverbs) 1:7*

A child has a natural, unconditional love and adoration for his father, especially during the earliest years of life. Accompanying that love is a healthy fear, one that responds immediately when the tone of his father's voice changes to convey concern or reproof. This is how the child begins to learn where his boundaries are—where he is protected, and where he is in danger. He may not understand *why* these things are so, but for a while at least, he accepts them as truth.

Such is the *"beginning of knowledge."* That *"fear of ADONAI"* keeps us on the path as we begin to learn how to walk in righteousness and holiness. It always seems, however, that as we gain the knowledge of God, we begin to think we know as much as He does. We believe we have the right to not only question, but to choose alternatives to His ways.

Enter: the fool. Wisdom comes from a single source alone, and that is ADONAI. To despise wisdom is to reject ADONAI. We mistakenly believe that one is mature in the faith if he has *knowledge* of the Scriptures and appears to be able to make godly decisions. But true

Messianic Daily Devotional **51**

wisdom is upheld by discipline. An unwise man leads an undisciplined life—he is tossed about by his own perceptions and emotions, and fails to consult the one from whom all true wisdom flows.

Discipline is not a prize to be attained, or a trophy that can be displayed on a mantle. Discipline is the foundation for personal growth and maturity in Messiah, and it manifests itself as a consistent string of fruitful decision-making. One is not disciplined because he keeps this commandment or that commandment, nor because he can quote an appropriate Scripture for every occasion. Discipline is having the personal integrity to sit in healthy fear before the Lord and wait for *Him* to speak, and to not move until He does. When we fail to seek the voice of God—and to wait until we hear it— we will make decisions according to our own wisdom... which is really nothing more than foolishness.

ॐ ॐ

Abba, Father, let me hear Your voice today. I commit to You now that I will go no further along this path until You give me clear, explicit instructions. I know that You show Your people the end from the beginning, but all I ask for now is the next step. ADONAI, help me to never lose my fear of You, but to always seek Your wisdom and discipline. Grow me, Father, and then show me how to move on from here....

When You Say My Name

"He who overcomes—this one—shall be arrayed in white garments, and I will not blot out his name from the scroll of life. I will confess his name before my Father, and before His messengers." Revelation 3:5

That's a line I'd stand in forever—I'd wait my turn as long as it takes… Can you *imagine?* You stand before the Creator of the Universe as the Messiah Yeshua *personally* announces your name, and it is heard by the Father and all of the heavenly host—you are acknowledged and recognized, now an eternal being….

Can it get any better than that?

What glory do we seek for ourselves here on earth? What things do we pursue in order to bring us minor fame and acknowledgment among people? We fail to realize that life in Messiah carries with it the greatest of all rewards! Not only can we live an abundant and joyful life today, but we can also look forward to our individual acknowledgment in Heaven—not just a nod, not just another name read in quick succession among countless others, but a significant, profound moment of recognition in front of all the heavenly beings. This is the greatest fellowship of all time… an eternal moment when the God of Creation, His Son, and all of Heaven and Earth have a singular, personal, intimate exchange with *you*—only you.

Is this what fame is all about? Is this the same kind of recognition we seek from our peers, our families and friends—and worst of all, from strangers? No, this is the "fame" that we can only dream about. It is not vain; it is not conceited—it is the single most humbling moment for the redeemed eternal.

If you know the Messiah Yeshua—if you walk in His ways; if you are pure and spotless, worthy to be dressed in white; if you find your victories only along the path of God—then this is your destiny. And the beauty is that, in that moment, you will not feel an ounce of pride or arrogance. You will not be thinking of yourself at all, when, at the sound of your own name, you bow down before the God of the Universe, pressed down under the weight of your own humility at the ultimate moment of total and final holiness.

Does the Lord *ever* stop *giving*?...

ૐ ૐ

Father of Creation, I cannot fathom what it will be like to stand before You and to hear Your Son speak my name in Your presence. Teach me how to be pure, blameless and holy before You right now. Show me how to bow myself before You daily; help me to remember that You deserve all the glory, all the praise, and all the honor... and that only *You* are famous. Father, turn my humiliation to humility, and prepare me for my garment of white....

Smooth Things

"*Now, go in, write this on a tablet for them, and engrave it in a book, and it will be for a later day, for a witness to the age: that a rebellious people is this, sons—liars, sons not willing to listen to the* תּוֹרָה, *Torah of* ADONAI—*who have said to seers, 'Do not see,' and to prophets, 'Do not prophesy to us straightforward things; speak to us smooth things. Prophesy deceits, turn aside from the way, turn away from the path. Cause to cease from before us the Holy One of* יִשְׂרָאֵל, *Yis'rael.'"* יְשַׁעְיָהוּ *Y'sha'yahu (Isaiah) 30:8-11*

People love to be told what to do—as long as it's what we want to hear. We are more than willing to submit to authority and live by the letter of the law, as long as the restrictions placed on us don't conflict with whatever we want to do. As human beings, we are naturally rebellious. We want what we want, when we want it, and we don't like it when we don't get our way. In fact, we will fight against any force that would have us behave contrary to our desires in an attempt to convince them to comply with our demands.

As an excuse for our behavior, we look for validation from those in authority. Yet, we find no validation as long as policy stands in opposition to our practices. So we cry out to those who are responsible to watch out for us, "*Do not see!*" To those who would challenge us in the ways we live, we say, "*Do not prophesy to us straight-*

forward things!" If they would only do as we ask, all would be well—surely, our whole-hearted obedience would be forthcoming.

The rebellious heart desires to *"turn aside from the way, turn away from the path,"* and to take everyone around with it. Rebellion hates solitude, and finds its solace in the company of other rebels. To this end, the rebellious one will lie, deceive and defy the truth—all for his own fulfillment and consolation. When we give in to the rebellious heart, nothing short of its complete satisfaction will suffice.

As disciples of Messiah, we can no longer ask the prophet to *"speak to us smooth things"*—to tell us only what we want to hear. Now that sin has been defeated in our lives, we must no longer give in to the heart of rebellion or the prophecy of deceits. We must be sons *"willing to listen to the Torah of ADONAI"* so that the Holy One of Yis'rael will not be caused to *"cease from before us."*

Let *our* testimony be a *"witness to the age:"* that we asked the prophets to *"prophesy to us straightforward things"*—and we listened....

ॐ ॐ

To the seers I say, "See!" To the prophets I say, "Speak to me challenging things," that I may fully know ADONAI and follow in all of His ways for all of my days. I praise You, ADONAI, for taking from me my rebellious heart, and giving me a heart that desires only to serve You and to do Your will. I bless You, my God, Holy One of Yis'rael, Author of the straightforward things...

Double Talk

"Once has God spoken, twice I heard this,
that 'strength is with God.'" תְּהִלִּם *T'hillim*
(Psalms) 62:11

Usually when God speaks to us, we don't even hear
half of what he's saying—if we hear anything at all. With
the multitude of distractions around us, it is often a
struggle to process, comprehend and apply what the
Master is saying. Much of what He says goes in one ear
and out the other, so that we retain only a vague
silhouette of truth.

The Psalmist puts is quite elegantly: *"Once has God
spoken, twice I heard...."* What God speaks is powerful
—it is mighty to change us if we will grab hold of it with
unusual tenacity. If we will just embrace His words, they
will impact us as if He had said them again and again.

But all too often, ADONAI has to speak the same
thing to us repeatedly until we finally get it. We wonder
why we continue going around in circles; we get depressed
when we feel we are not being delivered from the raven-
ous cycles of life... and this speaks to the quality of
interaction we have with the Father. We are so busy
trying to prove our ability to fix our own problems that
we just let God ramble on, not taking the time to listen
to a word He says. In His grace, He continues talking—
even when we have tuned Him out.

To hear what God is speaking once, we need to
deliberately be quiet and still. To hear it twice, we need

to deliberately *stay* quiet and still—even when we think we have important things to do. If we can only spare fifteen minutes a day with the Lord, we better stay thirty. If we can only spare thirty minutes a day with the Lord, we better stay sixty. "*Strength* is *with God*," and He wants to pour it into you—if you can just wait until the second half…

ॐ ॐ

Abba, give me the peace to know that everything else can wait—You come first. Teach my heart and mind to be quiet and still before You, and then show me how to stay in that place of listening to Your voice. Abba, I worship You; I am here on my face before You. Help me to not move until I have heard all that You are saying to me today…

It's Dirty Work, But Somebody's Got to Do It

"*Without oxen a stall is clean, but great is the increase by the power of the ox.*" מִשְׁלֵי *Mish'lei (Proverbs) 14:4*

It ought to humble us to know that ADONAI has chosen mere humans to accomplish His great will upon the earth. Like the ox, "*great is the increase by the power*" of people—especially when we are all pulling together in the same direction. But along with that strength comes a lot of stuff that just really stinks and makes a big mess. Why has ADONAI chosen such a beast of burden as man?

Why doesn't the Lord prefer to do His work by Himself? Indeed, "*without oxen a stall is clean.*" The very presence of man leaves a stain wherever he goes—and for all the good that he may do, there is always something left to clean up. Wouldn't it be better for ADONAI to set man aside and treat him as a dumb animal, left to his own uncleanness and base existence?

Instead, ADONAI esteems us—He lifts us up, and in spite of the waste we create, He sees great value in the work that we do. Our ability to produce results for the kingdom of God outweighs the nasty stuff that accompanies it. ADONAI would rather have filthy stalls filled with hard-working oxen, than have empty and spotless booths while He does all the work Himself.

We would do well to remember this as we deal with our fellow believers. We are all pulling together toward the same goal. And as we go, we sometimes make a big pile of stuff that other people will trip on, fall in, or have to step around. We need to remember to clean up after ourselves—but if we can't, there are others around to help us. We also need to remember that whenever we step in someone else's stuff, there is probably someone stepping in ours, too. We all put our pants on one leg at a time, and we all make a mess in our stalls. And the Lord still wants us. Now *that's* love.

ॐ ॐ

Father, thank You for loving me even when I make a mess. Thank You for using me even though I stink things up. Teach me, Lord, to be more aware of how I am treating others in Your kingdom. Help me to be a sweet fragrance to those with whom I serve. I praise You, Abba, that You have taught me what it means to be clean—and that You want me and love me even when I am not.

Escape or Salvation?

"[Yeshua said,] 'Now my soul is in turmoil,
and what? Will I say, "Father, save me from
this hour"? But [it is] because of this I came to
this hour. Father, glorify Your Name!' Then
out of heaven there came a voice [saying], 'I
[have] both glorified [it], and will glorify it
again...'" יוֹחָנָן *Yochanan (John) 12:27-28*

Our natural escapist mentality tells us that we need to get out of this world as soon as we can—to escape from the hardships and difficulties of this life and into Heaven's arms. When we were born again, God gave us a built-in desire to want to be home with Him. Yet we often forget that our salvation is not limited to being saved from death—it is also being saved from a dismal and defeated life. Yeshua, our salvation, is not merely our point of reference when aiming at Heaven, but our Rabbi—our teacher of how we are to live *today*. Yeshua, by his example, teaches us how to receive our salvation in *now* terms.

So what does it mean to experience salvation *now*? Consider the Master in His most desperate hour. Would not the Father be willing to save His Son from turmoil? Is not a loving Father more interested in the comfort of His child than His own glory? And yet, instead of asking for relief, the Master offers a sacrifice of praise: *"glorify Your Name!"*

In His greatest turmoil, Yeshua demonstrates prophetic praise—He is aware of His present circumstances, yet sees past them to His ultimate destiny. By being aware of the Father's heart and plans for Him—the very definition of being prophetic—Yeshua could see that His *present* circumstances were not only temporary, but were directly along the path that led to His ordained purpose. He was able to see the *value* of perseverance, because the payoff for His determination would be the greatest glory of all.

Not asking for salvation from the *present* turmoil can bring glory to the Father at a time in the *future*. Perhaps we shouldn't be so quick to ask for salvation from our circumstances just because we can't see the end from the beginning. Our greatest fulfillment is to see *the Father* glorified—and sometimes, it may very well be our perseverance that leads to His glory.

The Father has plans for us, and His reasons will bring us to our most profound crossroads. We just have to decide if we are going to take the path of comfort, or the road of glory.

ॐ ॐ

Abba, reveal to me my destiny, that I may persevere toward the goal that You have set before me. Even when I cannot catch a glimpse of my future, Father, give me the determination to press on for Your glory. Increase my strength and courage in You, so that I can stand firm even when all my senses are telling me to run away. Yeshua, You are my Master, and I receive Your salvation *now*. I praise You, ADONAI, and I desire only to bring glory to Your Name....

No Fear

"In this, love has been made perfect with us, that we may have boldness in the Day of Judgment, because even as He is, we—we also are in this world. Fear is not in love, but perfect love casts out fear, because fear has punishment, and he who fears has not been made perfect in love." אָ יוֹחָנָן *Yochanan Alef (1John) 4:17-18*

Take a deep breath. Really—try this: take a deep breath in… now let it out. Take another deep breath in… now let it out. What do you suppose are the chances that if you tried to take another deep breath, you would suddenly stop breathing? Is it likely? Let's see… one more time, take a deep breath in… now let it out. That's amazing, isn't it? We're *still* breathing!

Shouldn't we be surprised that this is the case? After all, is it by our own strength and our own will that we wake up every morning, breathe, live, lay down at night and wake up again the next day? No. It is the Spirit of God who gives us that first breath… and the next and the next and the next. And yet, each breath comes as no surprise at all—indeed, we take it for granted that ADONAI sustains our lives.

And still we wonder… "ADONAI, are You paying attention over here? I'm getting a little stressed, in case You didn't notice. There don't seem to be enough hours in the day, Father, and You *still* expect me to pay attention to my family? I could really use *Shabbat* to catch up on work, God, what do You say, huh? Just this *one* Shabbat, Father? Yes, Lord, You're on the throne. No, Lord, we've never gone hungry. Yes, Lord, You promised in Your Word You would provide for me, and You've never let me down, but... *it doesn't look to me like we're going to make it this time!*"

"*...perfect love casts out fear, because fear has punishment...*" Of what are we afraid? That God will turn His back on us? That He will leave us for dead, exposed to the elements? Yeshua didn't just buy our salvation in the hereafter; He paid for our freedom— our protection from punishment and fear—*today.* There's certainly plenty out there to fear, but the Good News is that for those who are in Messiah Yeshua, we are no longer "out there" but *brought near.* Here in Messiah, there is no punishment—there is only His perfect love... and that is why there can be *no fear.*

༚ ༚

Abba Father, make me strong when I am weak; remind me of Your salvation when I can't see past my present circumstances. Lift me up in Your love so that I will no longer need to *see* to believe. With every breath, Master, remind me of your goodness; in every Shabbat, teach me of Your peace. Show me perfect love, that I may be whole in You... free from fear, unafraid of punishment, and confident in Your ability—and Your desire—to always, always, *always* save...

Is It Me?

"'The sons are gathering wood, and the
fathers are causing the fire to burn, and the
women are kneading dough to make [sacrifi-
cial] cakes to מְלֶכֶת הַשָּׁמַיִם, M'lechet HaSha-
mayim, [the sun, the moon, and the stars,]
and to pour out drink-offerings to other gods,
so as to provoke Me to anger. [But is it] Me
they are provoking to anger?' ADONAI declares,
'[Rather,] is it not themselves [they are
hurting]—to the shame of their own faces?'"
יִרְמְיָהוּ Yir'm'yahu (Jeremiah) 7:18-19

ADONAI, the living God, does not require food and
drink for sustenance. How much less do the sun, the
moon, and the stars—His inanimate creation? And yet
we deprive ADONAI of the offerings and sacrifices He
desires from us, instead giving our devotion and service
away to other "gods." When we redirect our allegiance,
misplace our trust, and demonstrate our disobedience
through offerings made to the "gods" of our lives, we
provoke ADONAI to anger. But when we do this, who are
we really hurting?

"[Is it] Me they are provoking to anger?" queries
ADONAI. Surely, He has every right to be angry when we
steal from Him His rightful due; and, indeed, angry He
becomes. But is that all there is to the story? What happens when we focus on our wants and desires, relegat-
ing the Lord to just a small corner of our busy lives?
Why does ADONAI's anger flare up when we display our

adoration for other so-called gods—"gods" that demand our time and resources, yet are wholly unworthy to receive such loyalty?

When we steal our devotion from ADONAI and give it to other "gods," we are not wounding Him—we are hurting ourselves. His anger does not flare up because we've injured Him in some way. He is angry because His children are being led away from His protection and mercy—and we go along with it as willing participants.

We "shame [our] own faces" when we turn away from ADONAI—we are rejecting the One who not only truly cares for us, but who alone has the inclination *and* the real power to give us life. ADONAI is not some flaming ball of gas or orbiting rock in the sky, mindless and unable to save. He is alive—the living God! And unlike the "gods" we create, thinking they will keep us safe, He alone can save us from harming ourselves…

ॐ ৵

ADONAI, the Living God, forgive me for not giving You the devotion due Your Name. Teach me to devote myself fully to You, that I will not divide my attention between You and the "gods" of my own creation. I praise You, ADONAI, for You alone have the will and the power to save. You are my God, ADONAI—keep me from harming myself, that I may serve only You for all the rest of my days…

I Am Worn Out With Groaning

"...O ADONAI, in Your anger, reprove me not, nor in Your fury chastise me. Favor me, O ADONAI, for I am weak, Heal me, O ADONAI, for troubled have been my bones, and my soul has been troubled greatly, and You, O ADONAI, till when? Turn back, O ADONAI, rescue my soul, Save me for Your kindness' sake. For there is no remembrance of You in death, in שְׁאוֹל, Sh'ol, who will give thanks to You? I am worn out with groaning, I make my bed swim through all the night, with my tears I drench my couch. My eyes grow weak with sorrow, they fail because of all my adversaries. Turn from me all you workers of evil, for ADONAI [has] heard the voice of my weeping, ADONAI has heard my supplication; ADONAI [has] received my prayer. All my enemies [will] be ashamed and greatly troubled, they [will] turn back—ashamed in a moment!" תְּהִלִּם T'hillim (Psalms) 6

King David experienced intense inner turmoil, just as many of us have been known to do. But here in the sixth psalm, the man of God teaches us how to pull up out of an emotional tail-spin before spiraling into self-destruction.

"O ADONAI, in Your anger, reprove me not..." David's first priority is to get his bearings—he looks to the Father to find out where he stands… to make sure he is right with God. By first looking *upward*, we are able to look *inward* to see if everything is as it should be.

"Turn back, O ADONAI, rescue my soul…" Realizing he has no control, David reaches out to the Lord. He sees his desperate need and his total inability to save himself. He relinquishes his own strength and turns to the One who is the source of true power. ADONAI alone is able—and willing—to save us.

"I am worn out with groaning…" Completely spent and totally depressed, this is the point of giving up. This is where we concede our failures, accept our fate, and collapse—hopeless, beyond help. Yet even though he has reached his wits end, David puts his trust in the One who loves him—the One who is watching out for him and taking care of him, even when David is too exhausted to notice. Now it's up to the Father… it's all in His hands.

"Turn from me all you workers of evil…" Spiritually renewed, David awakens from his stupor and jumps right into spiritual warfare. Totally broken, with not a shred of ego left, he finally sees the spiritual reality of his situation. Although he has no strength to defeat his enemies, he is protected by the only One who can turn them back *"in a moment"* in shame.…

&⌇ ⌇&

ADONAI, my God, teach me to turn only to You in times of trouble. When I am distressed, remind me that You are my Salvation. Help me to see the spiritual reality of my situation… Am I right with you? Am I being spiritually oppressed by powers that I cannot see? Teach me, ADONAI, that You alone can save—and not just that you are *able*, but You are *willing*…

Let Me Finish My Life First

"*...And Yeshua said to another, 'Be following me;' and he replied, 'Master, permit me to go away first to bury my father;' and Yeshua said to him, 'Send away the dead to bury their own dead, and you, go away, proclaim the kingdom of God.' And another also said, 'I will follow you, Master, but first permit me to say "good-bye" to those in my house;' and Yeshua said to him, 'No one having put his hand on a plough and looking back is fit for the kingdom of God.'"* Luke 9:59-62

There's just no pleasing this Messiah... this Yeshua! When I say I will follow Him, He expects me to follow Him *now*! When He commands me to come, I'm more than willing—all I'm asking for is a little time to make the adjustment.... *Suddenly*, I'm not fit to serve just because I'm thinking a little bit about *myself*?

Excuses, excuses. Some may even appear to be reasonable—sensible—to our natural minds. This is often a hang up for us as disciples of Messiah: Does following the Lord *really* have to be so cut and dry?... So black and white?... Amen!!! Life in Yeshua is as black and white as night and day—the kingdom of darkness and the kingdom of Light.

When we make excuses to the Lord, are we trying to avoid future consequences, or are we merely holding onto something we don't want to give up? Take a look at the first fellow, so concerned for his dying father. Indeed, had his father already been dead, he would have been home, most appropriately, "sitting *shiv'ah*" (mourning). But his *true* motivation was to sit at home in *comfort, waiting* for his father to *die* so he could receive his inheritance and join Yeshua *at his leisure*! Comfort, ease, contentment... not evil in and of themselves, but what about when they become more important to us than following Yeshua?

Are we pursuing the Master, or making excuses? Are we following, or procrastinating? Does all of this mean that we have to abandon our lives, leave our jobs and lose all sense of security? For some, yes! But for most of us, not making excuses simply means deliberately listening to the Lord's leading, submitting our lives to the Scriptures... and just doing it.

გ• •დ

Father, I give up my life to You. You know what I need—You are my complete provision. My rest and comfort I find only in You. Convict me of my excuses and restore me to Your service. Teach me how to hear Your voice clearly—how to be sensitive to Your Spirit, and to be obedient to Your Word. I give You ownership of my life because I trust You completely. Thank You for taking care of me and showing me how to follow closer to You....

Nothing in the House

"A certain woman… cried to אֱלִישָׁע, 'Eliysha, saying, 'Your servant, my husband, is dead.… A creditor has come to take my two children to himself for servants.' And אֱלִישָׁע, 'Eliysha said to her, '…Tell me, what do you have in your house?' And she replied, 'Your maid-servant has nothing in the house except a pot of oil.' And he said, 'Go, ask for vessels for yourself… from all your neighbors— empty vessels—let them not be few. When you have entered [your house], shut the door upon yourself and your sons and pour out [oil] into all the vessels. Remove the full ones.' And she went from him, and shut the door upon herself and her sons. They brought [vessels] to her, and she poured out [into them]. And it came to pass, at the filling of the vessels, that she said to her son, 'Bring me another vessel,' and he said to her, 'There are no more vessels,' and the oil stopped. She went and told the man of God, and he said, 'Go, sell the oil and repay your loan, and you and your sons may live on the rest.'" מְלָכִים ב M'lachiym Beit (2Kings) 4:1-7

When the widow sought help from the man of God, his response surpassed all rational thought. But even though 'Eliysha's instructions made no apparent sense, the widow responded with faith and obedience—and in the end, she received an over-abundance of supply.

How willing are we to trust that God can perform outside and above natural reason and logic? In times of great need, will we trust that ADONAI has the power to save—that He will provide for our lack to the very last drop?

The widow had only one limitation in receiving all that God desired to supply. As 'Eliysha instructed, the widow gathered together as many containers as she could find—empty containers, and not just a few!—and she poured out into them. And the oil flowed, and flowed, and flowed, and flowed. Finally, when all the containers were full, *"the oil stopped."* Did the widow have just enough containers to hold all that God desired to supply, or did God stop pouring out His blessing because she had no more room to collect it?

What kind of containers do we have in our lives today? With what are they filled? Has God started pouring out blessings upon you, only to find that your many containers were already filled with other things —and *"then the oil stopped"*? God wants us to empty ourselves completely, so that He can fill us up with as much as we can hold. He will not only give us *enough*, but *more* than enough—and we will *"live on the rest."*

જી જી

ADONAI, I'm cleaning house today—Your servant has nothing in the house but a pot of oil. I am getting rid of all the junk, clutter, and garbage that's taking up space, and I'm making room for You to fill me up— permanently! Show me how to keep my heart and mind clear of those things that are not of You, that I will always have empty containers to receive Your abundance. Pour out Your oil today, Father! Thank You, my Master, for filling me up to overflowing....

What Right Do You Have?

"And to the wicked God has said, 'What
[right] do you have to tell of My statutes? That
you lift up My covenant on your mouth? Yes, you
have hated instruction and cast My words behind
you. If you see a thief, then you are pleased with
him—with adulterers is your portion. Your mouth
you have sent forth with evil, and your tongue
joins deceit together. You sit and speak against
your brother—against a son of your mother [you]
give slander. You did [these] things, and I kept
silent. You have thought that I am like you, [but]
I rebuke you, and set [these things] in order before
your eyes. Understand this now, you who are forgetting God, lest I tear [you to pieces] and there
[be] no deliverer: He who [offers] a sacrifice of
praise honors Me. As to him who orders his way,
I [will] cause him to look on the salvation of
God!'" תְּהִלִּם T'hillim (Psalms) 50:16-23

Can the wicked know God's laws? Apparently, yes.
Not only can he know them, but he can even *understand*
them—at least enough to proclaim and lift up God's
"*covenant on [his] mouth.*" But even though one may
thoroughly know the laws of God, at the same time he
may be totally oblivious to the Lawgiver Himself—he
may know God's statutes, but he *forgets God.*

The Word of God has no affect on the one who does not know the Author, and such a person will be betrayed by his actions. Simply having knowledge of God's Word does not keep one from thievery, adultery, malicious slander and the like. The reason for knowing the Word is to know the Author, for only He can change us and make us holy.

The greatest perversion of God's Word is to become so familiar with it (or think we are so familiar with it) that instead of allowing the Word to transform our lives, we begin to believe that God conforms to who we want Him to be. To the wicked God says, *"You have thought that I am like you"*—but to our surprise, He doesn't fit into our box. Instead, He will *"rebuke [us], and set [these things] in order before [our] eyes."*

The one who thinks that knowing God's Word is equivalent to actually knowing God has already forgotten Him—he will be torn to pieces, and there will be no deliverer. But the one who seeks the Author through His Word, his way will be ordered. He will change and be conformed to the ways of ADONAI—and will be caused to *"look on the salvation of God!"*

இ ஒ

Abba, Father, how I love Your Word. May I never pursue your statutes more than I pursue You. As I read Your Word, O God, teach me more of You; draw me closer to You and show me what it means to give You sacrifices of praise. I invite You to reside in the most prestigious place in my heart. Thank You, not for the right, but for the privilege of proclaiming Your covenant…

"The purposes of a man's heart are *[like]*
deep water; but a man of discernment draws
them out." מִשְׁלֵי *Mish'lei (Proverbs) 20:5*

If *"the purposes of a man's heart* are *[like] deep water,"*
then what do we find in the shallow water? Where the
light penetrates with little effort, it is easy to see what is
near the surface. The problem is that most of us only
allow *superficial* things to float to the top of our hearts.
It is no wonder that deep, meaningful, honest relationships are so difficult to achieve—we're all afraid to get
our hair wet.

The true purposes of one's heart lie deep beneath
the surface, where light cannot travel and darkness
envelops all. Though truth and honesty have natural
buoyant tendencies, our real intentions weigh them
down, keeping them submerged in the black waters.
Even the most discerning person cannot see that far
down, for no light can reach them. Though the
transparency of water hides nothing, the depths defy
perception and the purposes of the heart go unseen.

But *"a man of discernment draws them out."* The
discerning person knows where the real intentions lie,
and he dives into the depths to retrieve them. Grasping
in the shadows below, he takes hold of the heart's
purposes with one hand and swims upward with the
other. The closer they get to the surface, the more is
discovered; and the intentions of the heart are drawn
out of the water, laid on the beach, and resuscitated.

Truth and honesty spring forth, and all is revealed in the light.

Discernment loosens the grip of the heart's purposes on those things we would try to keep hidden. Truth, good or bad, always wants to rise to the surface—even when the purposes of the heart drown it in the deep. Let us not be content to either accept or display what is found in shallow waters, but let us determine to show our true intentions without the need for a search and rescue…

☙ ❧

Father, help me to not be a shallow person, but to allow the true purposes of my heart to rise to the surface —exposed for all to see. Teach me to not hide my true self away; help me to come into the light and be set free from a life of secrecy. I praise You, Abba, for showing me the ways of discernment, that I may help others to be drawn out of darkness and into Your light. I bless You, my God, for not leaving me to drown, but pulling me to safety….

How Blessed You Are

*"[How] blessed you are whenever [people]
insult you, and persecute [you], and say any
evil thing against you falsely for my sake. Rejoice
and be glad, because your reward is great in
the heavens, for in the same way, they persecuted the prophets who were before you."*
מַתִּתְיָהוּ *Matit'yahu (Matthew) 5:11-12*

The concept of Biblical blessing is generally associ-
ated with abundant living—having things like long life,
health, happiness, family, or a good return for our work.
But in this passage, Yeshua teaches us that we are blessed
when an abundance of insults, persecution, and false
accusations are heaped upon us. Why does He call us
blessed? Because we are following Him.

On one hand, we should be asking ourselves, "Am I
giving people anything about which to insult me? Am I
living my life so totally sold-out to Yeshua that persecution is coming against me?" The inherent nature of being
completely and humbly submitted to ADONAI should
cause the people around us to stir—yet all too often,
our spheres of influence remain largely unaffected by
our presence. Are we truly living as effective disciples of
Yeshua if no one ever pays us any attention?

On the other hand, the moment that persecution
begins, we should ask ourselves, "Who is provoking

these people to say and do such terrible things against me? Is it really Yeshua living through me, or am I bringing this on myself because I am a poor representative of the Master?" While a lack of persecution may be evidence of an ineffective walk with Yeshua, the abundance of persecution is not necessarily evidence that people are seeing the Master in us. We have to constantly check our humility meters, making sure that we start each day at the feet of the Master, rather than atop the thrones of our own making.

The prophets of old were insulted, persecuted and lied about—this is the fruit of abundance that we should also expect if we are living lives suited for the reward of Heaven. A life dedicated to Yeshua is one of intolerance for sin and separation from ungodliness. By virtue of living a sanctified life, we can expect that others will come against us in an attempt to return us to our former ways. We are blessed when we withstand the attack and press on unrelentlessly.

છે ન્

Abba, teach me to be humble—show me the ways of humility, that I may have confidence that You are the One people see in me. Help me to endure persecution that is for Your sake—but also allow persecution that is not for your sake to humble me and break me, so that You can pick me up and re-fashion me according to Your will. I bless Your Name, for You are the one who gives blessing. I rejoice in You, Yeshua, giver of Heaven's rewards....

Invisible One

"For having regarded the disgrace of the Messiah [as] greater wealth than the treasure in Egypt, [Moshe] looked [ahead] to [his] reward. By faith he left Egypt behind, not having been afraid of the wrath of the king... [instead,] he [remained] steadfast because [he had] seen the Invisible One." עִבְרִים *Iv'riym (Hebrews) 11:26-27*

What a strange way God expects us to walk: by faith. He has given us eyes to see and ears to hear, yet He wants us to forget them both—as if that were even possible. Surely a blind man needs at least a cane, but we are expected to walk without aid, leaning only upon our trust and hoping we will not stumble and fall. If we have sight and the sense of hearing, why shouldn't we be using them? Why were we given eyes, if not to see? Ears, if not to hear?

But since we *can* see, hear, taste and touch, what good would faith be if it required the use of our senses? Faith was designed to work under very specific conditions: in the dark, in the din, where our own senses fail. All too often, we rely on ourselves, thinking that we have everything we need to navigate through the obstacle course of life. We don't realize that in spite of our senses, we spend most of our lives stumbling from crisis to crisis. What we *need* is the faith to ignore what's standing in our way.

Moshe left Egypt behind *"by faith,"* meaning that he left *in spite* of the potential wrath of Pharaoh. Moshe could have given in to the perceived threat to his life and the lives of all the people of Yis'rael. Instead, he left Egypt without fear, because *faith* told him that there was nothing to worry about. By faith, we do not pretend there are no threats against us—but we are able to walk forward because we can *see* that they are really no threat at all. By faith, we do not allow what we perceive with our own senses to keep us from pressing on toward the reward that is ahead.

Moshe was able to stand fast in his faith *"because [he had] seen the Invisible One."* Like Moshe, we are also able to see Him every time we regard *"the disgrace of the Messiah,"* believing that this is *"greater wealth than… treasure."* Through Yeshua, we are able to walk forward, seeing the unseen, trusting our steps in both the light and the darkness alike. Faith teaches us to look ahead to our reward, and to walk in the confidence that we will receive it.

The Invisible One leads us daily—to follow Him, we need only to be willing to close our eyes….

ॐ ॐ

Invisible One, I praise You! Unseen Provider, You lay out a path before me. Thank You, ADONAI, for teaching me to walk by faith. Help me to trust only Your leading, and to not allow the threats and dangers of life to distract me. I bless Your Name, Father, because You alone are trustworthy and true. With blind eyes, I see You by faith, my Master—and I place all my hope in You….

Let the Boaster Boast

"This is what ADONAI says: 'Let not the
wise boast of his wisdom, nor let the strong
boast of his strength. Let not the rich boast of
his riches, but in this let the boaster boast: in
understanding and knowing Me, for I am
ADONAI, doing kindness, judgment, and
righteousness in the earth. For in these I have
delighted.'—an affirmation of ADONAI."
יִרְמְיָהוּ Yir'm'yahu (Jeremiah) 9:23-24

As we journey through life, there seems to be an
underlying motivation to accumulate—and our lives
reflect this. I remember a time in my life when everything I owned that was of any value could fit inside my
Plymouth Neon. Now my total number of possessions
can easily fill a 26-foot moving truck. Whether by greed
or necessity, our lives get filled up with stuff. That's
what happens.

Over time, we tend to not only fill our lives with
material possessions, but with intangible ones as well.
We seek knowledge, status, respect, acknowledgment,
spiritual fulfillment… "happiness." Yet after we have
collected all these things, to what do they really amount?
Can our lives truly be measured by our accumulations?
What value is there in our achievements?

To the wise, ADONAI says he should not *"boast of his wisdom;"* to the strong, he should not *"boast of his strength;"* and to the wealthy, he should not *"boast of his riches."* Instead, when we boast, we are to boast that we understand and know ADONAI. There is nothing else to which we have bragging rights. All our wisdom, all our strength, and all our wealth come from Him. These He bestows by His gracious hand—we did not collect them ourselves.

Without ADONAI, we truly have nothing. The things that have inherent value by the world's standards don't really have any value at all—except as a blessing from the One who is all-valuable. To understand and know ADONAI is to truly have everything one needs. Perhaps if we view our lives with this in mind, we will find that the things we previously held in such high regard are really not that important after all....

ॐ ॐ

Abba, Father, show me Your ways, that I may understand and know you—to know the things in which You take pleasure. Teach me to let my boasting be only in You, that I will learn what truly holds value in this life. I praise You, ADONAI, for You are not beyond understanding and knowing, but You give me the opportunity to understand and know You more every day....

Give Me Neither

"Two things I have asked from You, [do]
not withhold [them] from me before I die. Put
falsehood and lies far from me, [and] give [me]
neither poverty nor wealth. Provide me [only]
with the bread of my portion, lest I have too
much and deny [You], saying, 'Who is ADONAI?'
And lest I be poor, and steal, and profane the
name of my God." מִשְׁלֵי Mish'lei (Proverbs)
30:7-9

Is this a prayer of mediocrity? ...or worse, a con-
fession of unbelief that ADONAI has neither the ability
nor the *will* to bless His people? No, this is the prayer of
a person who wants to live a true and useful life—and
realizes that to do so, he must rely solely on ADONAI.

By wisdom or experience, this person has learned
that both poverty and wealth have a common disadvan-
tage: they can cause a person to take his eyes off God.
Our natural tendency is to be preoccupied with our
circumstances rather than devoted to ADONAI. In the
case of poverty, we are tempted to steal in order to
temporarily relieve our condition—and thus defile the
name of our God. In the case of wealth, we are tempted
to think more of ourselves than we ought, believing that
our riches were made by our own power—and thus
deny ADONAI's sovereign choice to pour out His
abundance upon us.

In hopes of avoiding both extremes, one simply
prays, "*provide me [only] with the bread of my portion...*"

But wait! Doesn't that sound too much like a hand-to-mouth existence? Where's the victory in that? The victory is in the *humility* and *faith* which comes from knowing that ADONAI takes all and gives all—from understanding that we do not lack or gain by our own strength or weaknesses. Lest we deny or profane the Holy One, it is better to live trusting him *daily* for our every need. This is the same truth the Master imparts by teaching us to pray, *"Give us today our daily bread…"* (Mat. 6:11)

The most dynamic life in Messiah is lived by those who walk along the straight and level path. This life is not an unpredictable game, full of mystery and surprises —it is a consistent experience of the peace, joy, and pleasure found through daily trusting the Lord. Yes, when He provides just the food we need today, we dwell in His presence—and we live enthralled with the anticipation that He will bring it again and again, new every morning.…

∾ ∽

God, my Father, as long as I live, keep falsehood and lies far from me. Teach me to live a true and useful life by relying solely on You for my every need. Abba, provide just the portion I need today, and I will be more than satisfied. I praise You, ADONAI, for Your provision is forever perfect. Help me to never deny or defile Your Name, all the days of my life.…

We Wait

"And let not this one thing be unobserved by you, beloved, that one day with אֲדֹנָי*, Adonai is as a thousand years, and a thousand years as one day.* אֲדֹנָי*, Adonai is not slow in regard to the promise, as some count slowness, but is patient with us, not willing any to be destroyed, but all to yield to reformation."* כֵּיפָא ב *Keifa Beit (2Peter) 3:8-9*

"When will You come?" I ask. He replies, "When I am done waiting for you."

Keifa teaches us that while leading lives of *"holy behavior and godly acts... waiting for... the Day of God,"* we must also hasten its coming (vs. 11-12). How amazing is it that as we wait and pray, eagerly looking forward to being home, He is actually waiting on *us* to hasten The Day? It is a source of great strength and confidence to realize that God's plan and purposes depend on *us* partnering with *Him* in his efforts—indeed, He designed it that way.

He waits for us, but He *"is not slow in regard to the promise, as some count slowness."* He waits because He loves us. He waits because He is patient. He waits for us to bring others into knowing His holiness... but more than that, He waits for *us*—you and me—to enter into His holiness *ourselves*! He waits for reformation. How long will He have to wait?

From our perspective, time is creeping along, with everything moving in slow motion. "Tomorrow" is inevitable to us—what we leave unfinished today, we'll always have time to do later. But to the Father, His children are racing toward their end. He sees the journey, the arrival, and the consequences all in the same instant—His wrath unleashed, His promises delivered—and, still, He waits, holding back until the very last moment. We wait for The Day, yet hope it will not come before *we* are ready.

Everyone should *"yield to reformation"* and turn from their sins… but will they? And if they don't, will it be because the Day of God came too soon? No! He is giving us every opportunity to lead lives *"holy in conduct and godly,"* and to hasten His coming. We hasten The Day by pursuing His purpose… and His purpose is that no one should be lost—least of all, ourselves.

We wait. He waits. Who will move first?

ॐ ॐ

Father, renew in my heart and mind the desire and passion for Your holiness and Your salvation, found only in Yeshua. Let the time of waiting be over, and let *me* be the first to move. How I long to be home with You, but I will continue to wait patiently while working to hasten Your Day. I praise You, worship You, and give You glory and honor, for You are wise and patient—and You are waiting on me.…

Forgive and Forget

"*And* דָוִד, *David said to* נָתָן, *Natan, 'I
have sinned against* ADONAI.' *And* נָתָן, *Natan
said to* דָוִד, *David, 'Also—*ADONAI *has caused
your sin to pass away; you will not die.'*"

שְׁמוּאֵל ב *Sh'muel Beit (2Samuel) 12:13*

Even one anointed of God can fall into sin, suffering immeasurable consequences—and yet he can also
be forgiven, washed clean, and then move on in the
Lord. King David, the one anointed by God as king of
Yis'rael, did *"evil in the eyes of ADONAI."* (vs. 9) He
sowed in the fields of temptation and sin, and reaped a
harvest of death.

Instead of leading his people as they went to war,
David stayed home. He put himself in a precarious position he should never have allowed, creating a climate
conducive to sin. Acting on temptation, David seduced
another man's wife, got her pregnant, and then put her
husband on the war front to meet his sure death. With
the husband murdered, David betrothed the woman,
and together they had a son.

The prophet Natan came to David. Though David's
obvious intention was to keep his sin hidden, Natan's
prophetic words brought it into the light. Immediately,
David recognized and repented for his sin before
ADONAI, and he was forgiven.

But that wasn't the end of the story. As restitution
for the life of the woman's husband, David's newborn

son was struck ill and died. During the illness, David *"prayed to God on behalf of the child,"* laid prostrate on the ground, and *"fasted and wept"* for seven days (vs. 16). But after the child died, David *"rose from the ground, bathed and anointed* himself, *changed his clothes, came into the House of* ADONAI, *worshipped, then went into his house and asked for bread—they placed [it] before him, and he ate."* (vs. 20)

Our God is a God of justice—He does not allow sin to be passed over. However, He also does not want us to wallow in our misery. When He forgives us, He forgives us—no more guilt, no more reminders, no little voice prodding, "Remember when you committed adultery with another man's wife, and then murdered him?" *That* is the voice of the enemy. The voice of God says, "You are forgiven... once and for all." And then, because it pleases Him, He just blesses us all over again.

"And David comforted Bat-sheva (Bathsheba) his wife, and went in to her, and lay with her, and she bore a son, and he called his name Sh'lomoh (Solomon); and ADONAI *loved him..."* (vs. 24)

ADONAI, You are a just God—You rightly expose my sin, even when I try to keep it hidden. Thank You, Lord, that You are a merciful and forgiving God, that Your love is abundant, and that my offenses will not quench Your love forever. Make me like David—cleanse me of my sins, and forgive me once and for all. Show me in Your wisdom that I am washed clean by Your righteousness—that I am purified and acceptable to worship You.

Something Useless

"There is something useless that has been done upon the earth—that there are righteous ones to whom things happen as if they were doing the work of the wicked, and there are wicked ones to whom things happen as if they were doing the work of the righteous. I say that this also is useless." קֹהֶלֶת *Kohelet (Ecclesiastes) 8:14*

We've all seen this and been frustrated by it. We throw up our hands and say, "Why? What's the point in *anything*?" We're especially affected by this phenomenon when bad things are happening to *us,* and our "enemies" seem to be going along just fine. "Hey, I thought *I* was the righteous one here—*he's* the one who all the bad stuff is supposed to be happening to… right?"

Who can really say why this is a reality of life? Why *do* things happen to wicked people as if they were righteous, while other things happen to righteous people as if they were doing the work of the wicked? There is one thing of which we can be sure—God knows what He's doing, and it's His call. Perhaps the righteous man is going through a time of purification; perhaps the wicked man is being set up for a great fall—who knows?

Surely, the wicked man gives no credit to God for his fortune, while the righteous one contorts in his affliction as he watches his foe prosper. If this ever happens to you, there is one very important thing to remember: *don't get bitter.*

In our frustration, especially when it is prolonged, we have a tendency to become bitter—bitter against God, bitter against our enemies, perhaps even bitter against everyone and everything in general. This is a trap in which we cannot afford to get caught. Such apparent injustice certainly seems senseless to us, but the Lord may have some other point in mind.

If we persevere through such affliction and endure the emotional and spiritual effects, we will surely see prosperity and blessing—and our enemies will receive their reward as well. Yet even in our frustration, we must not harbor bitterness toward our enemies, secretly praying and hoping for their demise as a consolation for our hardship. In the end, we will find no joy in their defeat. We are to focus only on ADONAI and look for His deliverance—and He is sending it even now.

Becoming bitter will only ensnare us and keep us from receiving our blessing. Bitterness that is born from frustration—this also is useless.

ॐ ॐ

Abba, Father, help me to not be bitter as my enemy prospers—show me the ways of patience and perseverance as I await my own deliverance. Lord, You know what You are doing, and I have complete and total faith that Your justice will be done. Thank You, Father, for teaching me the ways of righteousness. I bless Your Name, for You are worthy of all blessing, Deliverer of the Righteous....

Such a Bargain!

> "'Bad, bad!' says the buyer [about the
> goods he is purchasing], then goes on his way
> and boasts [about the bargain he received]."
> מִשְׁלֵי Mish'lei (Proverbs) 20:14

I went shopping with my wife at our local "Savers"
—a second-hand discount store—and I found a shirt I
really liked. I tried it on and came out of the dressing
room. After pulling and yanking on the shirt for a
minute, my wife duly informed me that the shirt itself
was lopsided. Yes, *lopsided*. What was my response,
admiring myself in the mirror? "But, honey, it's not *that*
bad—and besides, it only costs four dollars! Maybe I
can get them to give it to me for *two bucks...*"

She didn't let me get the shirt.

"'Bad, bad!' says the buyer [about the goods he is
purchasing.]" We have to wonder—if the stuff is so bad,
why does the buyer want it? Maybe it's because the stuff
is only "bad" for the advertised price, and it wouldn't be
so bad if it didn't *cost* as much. In other words, if the
seller is willing to settle for a lower *price*, the buyer is
willing to settle for a lower *quality*. But what happens
after the transaction is complete? Suddenly, the item
grows exponentially in value and worth, and the buyer
has "such a bargain" to brag about!

There's a big difference between living within our
means and settling for less than God's best. We don't
need to be foolish, spending money we don't have on

the most expensive product there is—but we also don't need to accept the lowest quality items just because we're comfortable with the price. This is a rule that we can apply to our life in Messiah. We do not have to settle for the *"bad, bad"* stuff in our lives. We have the ability to live in an abundance of joy, fruitfulness, peace, and victory!

Let us not be stingy when it comes to the cost of living the abundant life in Messiah. Don't say, "I will settle for my life the way it is, because I can't afford to give more of myself to the Lord..." Give all you have, and what you will gain will be far more than you could otherwise afford. You see, Someone left a gift certificate in your name at the checkout counter. All you have to do in order to redeem it is pay the difference *with every fiber of your being*—and then, you'll *really* have something to boast about....

తు ~

Lord, I praise You, because You have made the price of discipleship completely affordable. Father, teach me to be willing to pay You your due every day of my life. Abba, what I receive in return far outweighs what I give, for You have truly given me the better part of the deal. I bless Your Name, ADONAI, for You spared no expense in saving and calling me. Show me Your ways, O Lord, that I may live my life totally "sold-out" to You....

Authority and Power

"Behold, I give to you the authority to tread upon serpents and scorpions, and on all the power of the enemy, and nothing by any means shall hurt you…" Luke 10:19

We have power. We have authority. Why, then, do we fear the enemy? Indeed, why do we fear man? Not only can we engage the enemy, but we can *trample* him, be victorious over him—and more than that, remain *completely* unharmed.

Was this just a pep talk the Master was giving the disciples? Was he merely exaggerating to make a point? No. This is fact. We have been given this authority in Yeshua's Name!

And yet, it doesn't take much to rattle our cage— we flinch at the first sign of trouble. What will it be? A lie?… A threat?… and suddenly we're convinced that we're in over our heads and we might as well succumb. We can't see the end of a dilemma from the beginning; and when things appear to go awry, we get knocked off track, put up the white flag and beg for a truce. Unfortunately, the enemy takes no prisoners, and that white flag may as well be our burial sheet.

Our victory is at hand—in our personal lives, our family situations, our business dealings, everywhere! We need only to receive the authority and power given us, stand in the face of the enemy, challenge his lies, rebuke his threats, and trust in the power of the Word of God and the blood of Yeshua—trust in our protection, provision, and victory… to God be the glory!

Don't be deceived—our difficulties in the natural are reflections of the attacks against us in the spiritual. The best way for the enemy to obstruct our effectiveness for the kingdom is to attack us in the areas where we are most vulnerable. But when we focus on our problems rather than on the Lord, we are unable to discern the events taking place in the spiritual realm. It is only when we fix our eyes on Yeshua that we will be able to see the schemes of the enemy.

So be bold! What you see, you can defeat—you have been given the authority… and from this war, you will emerge unscathed.

ౚ ౚ

ADONAI, cover me with Your atoning blood and reveal to me the weapons at my disposal. When the enemy tries to attack, remind me of the authority You have given me. Help me to be victorious, for Your glory, that I may continue to serve in Your kingdom. I trust completely in the authority and power You have placed in me by the *Ruach HaKodesh*. Thank You, Lord, that You are with me in times of trouble….

Righteous Sinner

"…And ADONAI said to יֵהוּא, Yehu, 'Because you have done well, to do that which is right in My eyes—according to all that is in My heart you have done to the house of אַחְאָב, Ach'av—the sons of the fourth generation will sit for you on the throne of יִשְׂרָאֵל, Yis'rael.' But יֵהוּא, Yehu did not guard [himself and] walk in the תּוֹרָה Torah of ADONAI—God of יִשְׂרָאֵל, Yis'rael—with all his heart. He did not turn aside from the sins of יָרְבְעָם, Yarav'am that caused יִשְׂרָאֵל, Yis'rael to sin." מְלָכִים ב M'lachiym Beit (2Kings) 10:30-31

Yehu: anointed King over Yis'rael by a messenger of the prophet 'Eliysha. He put to death Yoram, king of Yis'rael; Iyzevel (Jezebel), the treacherous wife of the evil King Ach'av (Ahab); 'Achaz'yahu, king of Y'hudah (Judah); and all the descendents of Ach'av. He annihilated the worshippers and priests of Baal in their own temple, breaking down Baal's standing stone, demolishing the temple, and turning it *"into a latrine."* (vs. 27) Yehu performed these righteous acts according to the word prophesied by Eliyahu, however….

"Yehu did not guard [himself and] walk in the Torah of ADONAI… with all his heart. He did not turn aside from the sins of Yarav'am that caused Yis'rael to sin."

ADONAI does indeed honor our good works. He takes notice, and people are blessed because we do them—our children's children will be honored because of our righteous deeds. To do good works in the name of right-eousness is to accomplish "that which is right" from God's perspective.

But the life of Yehu teaches us a sad truth—we can perform righteous acts *and still be a sinner.* We can do good things *for* ADONAI, yet care nothing about Him. In truth, doing good works is easy—mindless, even—but to live wholeheartedly for the Lord... that takes some effort. By not following God's ways, Yehu remained a sinner—despite his great accomplishments in the Name of ADONAI.

So how will you be remembered? As someone who did great works for God... or as someone who turned aside from *every* sin and walked in the ways of ADONAI *"with all his heart"?*

&ℯℴ ℴ℘

ADONAI, teach me to love Your ways, and remind me that I cannot live by works alone. Let me never hope to be made righteous by the things I do, but let my good deeds pour out from my deep relationship with You. I repent for striving to do good in Your eyes when I should have been simply seeking Your face. Father, thank You for loving me, caring for me, and showing me how to walk in holiness before You—wholehearted, abiding in the commands of Your Word, not straying to the left or the right, but walking only in Your ways....

I Will Add To All Your Praise

"But I continually wait with hope, and [I will] add to all Your praise. My mouth recounts Your righteousness, all day long [it proclaims] Your salvation—I do not know the number. I come in the might of יְהוָה אֲדֹנָי, *Adonai* ELOHIYM, I recall Your righteousness—Yours only."
תְּהִלִּם *T'hillim (Psalms) 71:14-16*

When we are going through trials and tribulations, we cry out to our Abba for deliverance—or, at least, we should. Sometimes, the weight of life's problems drags us down to the point that we find it difficult to even petition the Lord. We cannot lift ourselves up enough to turn toward Heaven and ask for help. How can we preserve and protect our connection to God, so that in times of trouble, we do not forget how to approach Him—or, even, that He is still approachable?

On our descent into deeper difficulties, we often turn to prayer. "Help" is usually a popular word, along with "please." Occasionally, "why" and "me" might make it in there as well. But the Psalmist teaches us that along with our petition, there is to be a multitude of praise.

Which comes first, hope or praise? Wherever you are most lacking is the best place to start. The goal is to

"*continually wait with hope, and add to all [God's] praise.*"
Both are increased when we use our mouth to confess
His righteousness and salvation. Though they are beyond
numbering, we are to recount them "*all day long.*" It is
in this way that we increase our hope, because there is
no such thing as praising God too much. Empty praise
upon empty praise will only deflate hope—but our
praise is not empty, for we have much to recount. The
key is to let praise *build* our hope, and then to respond
to the hope we have by praising Him some more.

As we recall the righteousness of God, we will be able
to come in *His* might. He alone is worthy of praise, He
alone gives us hope, and He alone gives us the strength
to persevere and overcome. We do not endure by simply
crying out to God—anyone can do that, and they often
do. The difference lies in having the fortitude to praise
God even in the worst of circumstances… and to keep
adding to that praise.

ೊ ೋ

ADONAI, teach me how to always hope, and to keep
adding to Your praise. Abba, draw me closer to You, that
I may know You more and respond to Your salvation by
adding to Your praise. Help me, Father, to remember to
turn to You always—both in my joy and my sorrow. In
every circumstance, I will glorify You with praise, recalling
Your righteousness, Yours alone. Teach me, Adonai
ELOHIYM, to keep Your salvation on my lips all day long…

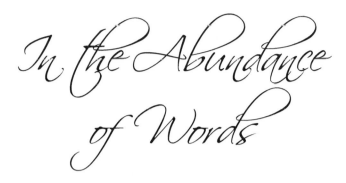

In the Abundance of Words

"In the abundance of words, sin ceases not; but whoever restrains his lips is wise.*"*
מִשְׁלֵי *Mish'lei (Proverbs) 10:19*

Do you have a tendency to dominate conversations? Do you often feel a need to wax eloquent, saying basically the same thing over and over again? When you are in a discussion or an argument, does the other person eventually succumb and get a glazed look in his eyes, as you continue to go on and on? Would you even notice if he did? Is it a regular occurrence for you to regret the things you have said, wishing that you could take them back? If you answered yes to any of these questions, you talk too much.

When we start running off at the mouth, we may very well be saying exactly what we feel, we may be totally honest and forthright—and we may even be absolutely correct. However, the problem is not necessarily with *what* we are saying, but with *how* and *why* we are saying it. Talking too much generally indicates a desire for control—an attempt to manipulate people or situations.

"In the abundance of words, sin ceases not...." The more we talk, the less control our new man has over our communication, and the message we are sending gets

twisted and distorted. By allowing our tongue to go untamed, we sin. Once unbridled, our tongue leads us into situations created out of our own flesh.

However, when we control our speech, we are exercising wisdom. This does not mean that we should purposely miscommunicate by saying something we don't mean, nor that we should hold back how we are truly feeling. It also does not mean that we can manipulate the situation by saying things we believe will get the other person to do what we want them to do—or think what we want them to think. Controlling our speech means that we only communicate what is upright and good—we deliberately filter out the things that cause confusion, hurt, or manipulation, and only allow the light of Yeshua to shine through.

When words abound, sin abounds as well—it fills our own lives and causes others to stumble. So let us restrain our lips, that we will be wise and effective communicators who transmit nothing but the love of Messiah…

இ ௸

Abba, Father, renew my mind and show me where sin is abundant in the many words I speak. Teach me, Lord, to control my speech—to not give my flesh any access to my tongue. ADONAI, show me how to rely only on You, that my words will never be self-edifying, but will always reflect Your true love and grace….

Temptation Leads to Life

"*Count* it *all joy, my brothers, when you fall into trials of many kinds; knowing that the testing of your faith works perseverance [in you]. Let perseverance have a maturing work, that you may be mature and complete—lacking nothing.... Happy [is] the man who perseveres [through] trials, because, becoming approved, he will receive the crown of the life which the Lord promised to those [who] love Him. Let no one being tempted say, 'I am [being] tempted by God,' for God is not tempted by evil, and [He] Himself tempts no one. Each one is tempted by his own desires, being led away and enticed. Afterward the desire, having conceived, gives birth to sin, and the sin, having been perfected, brings forth death.*" יַעֲקֹב *Ya'akov (James) 1:2-4, 12-15*

Life and death. We think of these as opposite destinies—and indeed, they are—but these two have more in common than we think. The roads that lead to life and death both intersect with a common path called temptation.

The way we handle temptation leads to two very different lives: the Life which God has promised, or a life of—and ending in—death. In both cases, temptation is the place where life begins—be it a Life for God or a life for Death. How we respond immediately following that moment of conception determines our path. To achieve death, it's a short trip—once securely fastened in the seat of temptation, next stop sin... and death is around the bend. But Life... how do you get *there*?

It takes determination to persevere through the tests of life and live! To live with Death, we only have to be *determined* to persevere in *sin*. But to live with God, we have to be *determined* to persevere in *faith*. Perseverance in faith makes us mature, complete and whole—it builds character. Perseverance in sin prepares us only for death.

We have a path to choose—but no matter what choice we make, God promises us life. If we persevere *in* temptation, pressing on toward sin, we will receive a life... of Death. However, if we persevere *through* temptation and head on toward faith, we *will* receive blessings and Life with God. Wholeness awaits on the other side of desire... so count it all joy!

૭ઽ ∾૭

Father, teach me to be quick to trust You and slow to embrace sin. Make me a person of character, that I will receive Life and the blessings You have promised to those who put their faith in You. Thank You, Father, that You are the restorer of all things—that even if I come to You in sin, You can set me on the right path. ADONAI, let me be determined to persevere in trust and holiness, pressing on toward You, that I might regard testing as joy—because You are waiting with the crown of life....

Obviously Oblivious

"'And I saw, when I gave יִשְׂרָאֵל*, Yis'rael the
document of divorce and sent her away (for all
the reasons whereby she backslid, committing
adultery), that treacherous* יְהוּדָה*, Y'hudah, her
sister, was not afraid, and went and prostituted
herself also. And it came to pass, from the vileness
of her fornication, that the Land was defiled, and
[*יִשְׂרָאֵל*, Yis'rael] committed adultery with stone
and with [pieces of] wood. Yet even in all this, her
treacherous sister,* יְהוּדָה*, Y'hudah, did not turn
back to Me with all her heart, but with false [pre-
tense].'—a declaration of* ADONAI*. And* ADONAI
said to me, 'Backsliding יִשְׂרָאֵל*, Yis'rael has shown
herself righteous, more than treacherous* יְהוּדָה*,
Y'hudah.'"* יִרְמְיָהוּ *Yir'm'yahu (Jeremiah) 3:8-11*

The northern kingdom of Yis'rael easily fell into sin
and became an adulterous wife to ADONAI. Her acts of
prostitution and whoring with other "gods" made her
worthy of the destruction she eventually received.
Yis'rael's sin spat in the face of her Beloved as she gave
herself to gods of the earth, her adulterous affairs with
stone and wood defiling the Land. Yis'rael did not merely
despise the blessings ADONAI had given her—she perverted them with her disgusting exploits of whoredom.

Yet ADONAI calls Yis'rael *"righteous, more than...
Y'hudah (Judah)."*

Though Yis'rael prostituted herself and ADONAI divorced her, Y'hudah's sin was far worse—far more vile, filthy and repulsive. Like Yis'rael, Y'hudah, *"went and prostituted herself also."* Y'hudah followed in Yis'rael's unfaithfulness and sinned because she *"was not afraid."* Though Y'hudah had a very obvious warning of ADONAI's wrath, she failed to fear what befell her sister. But even this was not Y'hudah's greatest sin.

More than following in unfaithfulness, more than not being moved to fear, Y'hudah's greatest sin against her Husband was her *"false [pretense]"* toward Him. In her depravity, Y'hudah was not only dishonest with her Husband, but she could not even be honest with herself. Y'hudah failed to see the obvious, and instead wallowed in her deep, dark oblivion.

Both Yis'rael and Y'hudah were adulterers, but Y'hudah compounded the sin when she made a false pretense of returning to ADONAI. More than sin itself, God despises being approached with unrepentance— and even more so when we are willful and unashamed, oblivious to our treachery. When we sin, let us be quick to repent with whole hearts, that our Husband will never send us away....

❧ ❦

ADONAI, I repent of my sins with all my heart. Father, set me free from the patterns that lead to destruction in my life—make me fear the consequences of sin, that I may never follow in another's unfaithfulness. Break me, Lord, so that You can heal me, and help me to never make a false pretense of returning to You. I praise You, Father, for You are forgiving and Your loving-kindness lasts forever. Thank You for receiving me again, Your beloved....

Let My Heart Be Undivided

"Show me, ADONAI, Your way, [so that] I [will] walk in Your truth; [let] my heart be undivided to fear Your Name." תְּהִלִּים T'hillim (Psalms) 86:11

All throughout the Psalms, the writer cries out to ADONAI, "Show me Your way." What does that mean? Does it mean, "Show me what You want me to do—and I will choose the things I like and reject the things I don't"? Does it mean, "Tell me how to get where You are—but show me grace while I make my own way to get there"? The Psalmist says, "show me Your way, [so that] I [will] walk in Your truth." How many "truths" does ADONAI have? Just one. So how many *ways* can He show us?

The all-paths-lead-to-god mentality of world spirituality also permeates the Body of Messiah. Surely we all move along the path of righteousness at different *speeds*, but ADONAI does not assign us each a different *path*— He does not allow us to work out our salvation in our own, personalized way. ADONAI's standards are set— immovable and immutable. His truth does not morph to accommodate us and our humanity—it is our humanness that must adhere to Truth's form and function. God's truth is fixed so that He can change hearts of stone into malleable, living flesh.

The Psalmist prays that ADONAI will make his heart "undivided." Since there is only one truth and one way to get to it, only a person with an undivided heart can submit to the ways of God and be changed. When we allow our hearts to follow after our own desires, when we let our life situations dictate the way to go, we do not have an undivided heart—we have given our heart to another.

We ask for an undivided heart so that we can fear His name. When we have multiple standards in our life, we have no true fear of God. Without His truth, there is always an alternate route we can take to avoid the things we don't want to encounter. But in the kingdom of God, there is one truth, one way, and only One Name to fear. To go our own way is to have no fear of God—and that takes us down another very distinct and very different path.

కఞ ఆఁ

For You are great, and You do wonders; You alone are God! ADONAI, show me Your way, so that I can live in Your truth; make my heart undivided, so that I can fear Your Name. I will praise You with my whole heart, ADONAI my God, and I will glorify Your Name forever! Your grace toward me is great, for You have rescued me from the lowest part of the grave....

Afterwards, Build

"Prepare your outside work, and make things ready on the land—then afterwards, go, build your house." מִשְׁלֵי *Mish'lei (Proverbs) 24:27*

Imagine you have just finished building and paying for your brand new dream house. You step foot into it for the very first time, and to your amazement, you find that the floor is sloping at a five degree angle. Somehow, the land was not adequately prepared—and, most astonishingly, no one noticed it until now. What do you do? The contractor has left with his last check (which is also *your* last check), your family is ready to move in, and your perfect house is on the verge of sliding off its foundation. Are you willing to tear down the whole house and start over, no matter what the cost?

Far more often than we would like to admit, we start down paths in our life that we eventually regret for one reason or another. Many times, we get so far down those paths that we think it is too late to turn back and start over again. Sometimes we find flaws in what we have built that can be fixed or covered over. But what do we do when we realize that the flaw is in the *foundation*—that we have built on unprepared land—and nothing will fix the problem short of tearing everything down and starting over from scratch?

Not only do we have to be willing to start over, but we have to then take the time to *"prepare [our] outside work, and make things ready on the land"* before we're ready to rebuild again. When the house comes down and you find yourself living in temporary dwellings again, all you can think about is putting that house back together—and the last thing you want to do is spend your time going over the land to make sure you get it right this time.

But this is the most important stage of the entire building project—especially when you realize what is truly being built: you. As we prepare and make ready the land, the Father is working in us patience, humility and trust—He is teaching us that in the end, the house stands or the house falls because He makes it that way.

Do you have any houses that need tearing down today? Let them fall, because ADONAI is about to build something the likes of which you have never seen.

ॐ ॐ

Abba, Father, make my heart ready for the house to come down. I want to do things right this time. Teach me to be patient as I work the land and prepare it for what is about to be built. I bless Your Name, O God, for You are the perfect builder, and I trust in You to guide me as I put my toil and sweat into this new home. Thank You, Lord, for entrusting me with this beautiful land—the house built here will be for You....

Don't Worry

> "And [Yeshua] said to his disciples, 'Because
> of this, to you I say, do not be anxious for your
> life, what you will eat; nor for the body, what
> you will wear; the life is more than the nourish-
> ment, and the body than the clothing.... Seek
> not what you will eat, or what you will drink,
> and be not in suspense... your Father knows
> that you have need of these things. But seek the
> kingdom of God, and all these things will be
> added to you. Fear not, little flock, because your
> Father delighted to give you the kingdom..."
> Luke 12:22-32

How many times can we read this passage and not
believe it? The Master exhorts us to ignore what we see
with our eyes and, instead, live our lives according to a
thing called "trust." Ironically, if we were to truly see
with our eyes—rather than through the distorted filter
of our fears—we would see the evidence of God's faithfulness and provision in the physical world around us.

If only we could hold onto that trust once and for
all, consider what we would receive: "Don't worry," "You
are worth much," "Don't be anxious," "Have no fear..."
Worry, fear and anxiety are anti-trust, anti-faith, and
anti-Messiah. Is Yeshua lying to us? Is the Shepherd
leading us astray? Of course not! And moreover, He is
not even asking us to believe in something we can't see
—God does *indeed* feed the birds, clothe the grass...
and, yes, He gives us the Kingdom!

Does it seem as if you repeatedly have to fight against your own insecurities to see the plain truth in front of your face? No rest for the weary? Here's how to overcome it: don't strive after your anxieties, but *"seek the Kingdom."* If you feel like you're constantly battling this issue of trust, you probably are. Do you ever find your mind focusing on or obsessing over a situation in which you have no control? Have you ever strategized for a potential confrontation with another person in your mind, trying to prepare yourself for all the contingencies—when, in reality, you don't really have any idea of what to expect from the other person? That's striving after your anxieties.

We allow our minds to fantasize about things that cause us great stress, yet freedom is available by simply changing our focus. Instead of feeding the black hole of worry—which returns nothing for your efforts—we need to look toward the Kingdom of God—which brings peace and a promise. If we can't trust Yeshua, then who can we trust? He is worthy of our faith—and He provides everything we need....

ॐ ∞

Father, I need to trust You more. Help me to have peace in my heart, and to not be anxious for anything. You have proven Your faithfulness to me over and over again. I know in my heart that You will never let me down, but sometimes my flesh tells me that I'm on my own. ADONAI, help me to resist the temptation to entertain such thoughts. I want to see only You... to seek only Your Kingdom. Thank You for Your faithfulness and all Your promises....

Sin, Repentance, Forgiveness

"'And in your spreading forth your hands,
I hide My eyes from you, Also when you increase
prayer, I do not hear, Your hands of blood have
been full. Wash yourself, make yourself clean,
Turn aside [from] the evil of your doings, from
before My eyes, Stop doing evil, learn to do
good. Seek justice, make happy the oppressed,
Vindicate the fatherless, contend for the widow.
Come, now, and we reason [together],' says
ADONAI, 'If your sins are as scarlet, as snow
they will be white, If they are red as crimson,
as wool they will be! If you are willing, and
have listened, The good of the land you [will]
eat...'" יְשַׁעְיָהוּ *Y'sha'yahu (Isaiah) 1:15-19*

"Wash yourself, make yourself clean, Turn aside
[from] the evil of your doings, from before My eyes, Stop
doing evil, learn to do good." A sinner's hands are covered
with blood because he repeatedly dives back into the
pool of transgression and iniquity. What can a sinner do
that will cause ADONAI to turn and listen? Repent. When
we repent, the blood comes off. Instead of appearing
before ADONAI with hands full of coagulating sin, we
stand before Him repentant and empty-handed. Yet the
stain colors deep. When we *"stop doing evil"* the flow of
blood is halted—the evil deeds are gone from the sight

of ADONAI and He can turn to us. He takes our dripping hands in His, and they are no longer covered with blood, but now clean.

"If your sins are as scarlet, as snow they will be white, If they are red as crimson, as wool they will be!" Now ADONAI—our hands in His—applies the forgiveness of sins to the stains on our hands. We are not only clean, but *restored*; and more than restored... *made new.* It is the atonement for sins that removes all evidence of our former ways. There is no stain to remind us—or ADONAI —of who we used to be. We are forever changed, a new creation, acceptable to the One who hears our prayers. Willing and listening, we now eat of *"the good the land."*

The Messiah Yeshua makes a way for us to receive this atonement permanently—once and for all. Until we turn to ADONAI, our hands are covered with blood. But when we repent, ADONAI hears our prayers, and our scarlet sins become as white as snow. We are made new in Messiah... forever.

ॐ ॐ

ADONAI, I praise You and thank You for removing the stains from my hands. I confess my sin to You, I repent and turn from my evil ways, and I freely accept Your atonement that gives life. I am new, and it is justice in Your eyes for me to receive Your blessings. I praise You, my King, for the abundance You have set before me. I know that all I need to remember is what You have done for me. Help me to listen and walk willingly, according to all of Your ways...

Still Keeping Hold

"And הַשָּׂטָן, HaSatan went forth from the presence of ADONAI and struck אִיּוֹב, Iyov with a sore-ulcer from the sole of his feet to [the top of] his head. And [Iyov] took to himself a shard [of pottery] to scrape himself with it, and he sat in the middle of the ashes. And his wife said to him, '[Why] are you still keeping hold of your integrity? בָּרֵךְ אֱלֹהִים וָמֻת, Barech 'Elohiym vamut. (Bless God and die.)' And [Iyov] said to her, 'You speak as one of the foolish women speaks. Indeed! [Shall] we accept the good from God, but not accept the evil?' In all this אִיּוֹב, Iyov had not sinned with his lips." אִיּוֹב Iyov (Job) 2:7-10b

It may be argued that there has been no one on earth other than Messiah who suffered more than Iyov. One of the great men of Scripture, we truly ought to consider him heroic, for ADONAI deemed him blameless and upright—and therefore worthy to suffer the affliction sent upon him. Indeed, because he was a model of faithfulness and fortitude, Iyov received personal attention from HaSatan himself.

Iyov lost oxen, donkeys, camels and servants to attacks from foreign thieves. He lost sheep to fire, and his children to the destructive forces of nature—all of them crushed in the eldest son's home by the force of a great wind. Iyov lost everything he owned, treasured or loved. He was ruined without cause. Many of us would be quick to see HaSatan as the reason for destruction in Iyov's life—and we would be right to do so. But the most unusual part of Iyov's story is ADONAI's role—everything done to Iyov was done with His consent.

Even more surprising than ADONAI's seeming conspiracy with HaSatan against Iyov is the fact that Iyov understood and—most shocking of all—accepted it. Sitting in a heap of ashes, scraping the sores on his body, surely mourning the loss of his family and all that he owned, Iyov refused to curse ADONAI. Iyov's wife, on the other hand, was quick to blame God—and to fault Iyov for holding fast to Him. But Iyov rebuked his wife and responded with conviction, saying, *"[Shall] we accept the good from God, but not accept the evil?"*

When we experience our own trials and suffering, we would do well to consider ADONAI's servant, Iyov. Iyov had every reason to blame ADONAI for his suffering and affliction, yet he held on to his integrity and instead chose to bless God in spite of his circumstances. Regardless of what we may think at times, ADONAI is not in league with the Adversary. Nevertheless, He does plan to put us to the test—not so that we will fail, but so that we can succeed. Will we still bless God when all seems lost and the only one left standing for us is Him?

ADONAI, You give, and You take away—but in either case, I will bless Your Name. Teach me to hold fast to my integrity, that regardless of my circumstances, I will be righteous toward You in all my ways. Let me not sin toward You with my lips, Abba, Father. Instead show me the ways of uprightness and blamelessness, that I may be one whom You single out for Your glory. ADONAI, I accept all your awesome ways, for You alone are God, and worthy of all my praise…

The Prayer of the Upright

"The sacrifice of the wicked is an abomination to ADONAI, but the prayer of the upright is His delight. An abomination to ADONAI is the way of the wicked, but He loves whoever pursues righteousness." מִשְׁלֵי Mish'lei (Proverbs) 15:8-9

The Scriptures encourage, exhort and teach us to pray—but never is prayer commanded. It is not a stipulation of any covenant; it is not a *mitzvah* (commandment) that can be kept or broken. We do not pray because ADONAI commands us to pray—we pray because it is part of our relationship with the Creator.

On the other hand, sacrifices are very much commanded—indeed, they are foundational to the system that brings redemption and reconciliation, now fulfilled in Messiah Yeshua. The need for sacrifices has not changed, only the conditions in which they can be made and accepted. So we continue to participate in the reality of the sacrificial system and temple priesthood through the Messiah.

And yet, "*The sacrifice of the wicked is an abomination to ADONAI.*" We can obey the Scriptures and do all that is commanded, performing deeds according to precise instructions—but if we are wicked, ADONAI will detest the crooked following of His own commands.

At the same time, *"the prayer of the upright is His delight."* We may fail to perfectly keep the commandments that ADONAI has laid before us—we may fall short and continue to miss the mark—but if we pursue righteousness with our whole heart, He will delight in our prayers… as inexact as they may be.

As we pursue righteousness, we will naturally pursue His commandments, for they teach us His ways—the ways of the upright. Prayer does not replace the need for obedience and sacrifice. Rather, it is the spiritual practice of an obedient and sacrificial heart… and in this, ADONAI finds pure delight.

ৈ৵ ৰ৩

Abba, I pray that this devotional time with You is delightful. I ask that You continue to teach me the ways of righteousness, that You will find great joy in me. Father, teach me Your ways, and show me who I truly am in You. ADONAI, I praise You and I bless Your Name. Holy One, thank You for hearing and loving my prayer…

While It Is Still Dark

"*And very early [in the morning,] while it was still dark, [Yeshua] got up, left, and went away to a solitary place, and there [He stayed] praying.*" Mark 1:35

When trying to follow the Master's example, it is easy to get discouraged if someone doesn't get healed, or another doesn't get saved, or we don't have enough faith, or we just can't seem to accomplish enough for the Kingdom. Then, the idea creeps into our minds that this is why He is the Master and we are the students—His level of power and effectiveness will always be unattainable. But that is exactly the *opposite* of what the Master teaches us. As we emulate Him, we should expect to operate as He did—and even to a greater degree!

As disciples of Messiah, we are supposed to be like the Master. But Yeshua, the Word of God, *is God*—how, then, can *we* be like the Master? There has to be more to it. There must be something in Yeshua's life to which we mere mortals can legitimately aspire. Indeed, *His* power and effectiveness was achieved by the very same means that is available to *us*—by relying solely on the Father, and turning to Him continuously in *prayer*.

In setting this example for us, Yeshua was not simply performing an outward act that ordinary human beings could imitate. Yeshua prayed because He *needed* to pray. He *needed* to connect with the Father. Why? To receive direction, to be revitalized, to get refocused. He prayed for the same reason we need to pray—without prayer, we will be unable to complete our mission. Without prayer, we are lost, because we cannot hear the voice of the Father.

Can we surmise that Yeshua knew the best time and place for individual prayer? Perhaps. While talking on the phone, have you ever switched extensions or moved to another room because external noises were keeping you from hearing the person on the other end? Why should prayer be any different? Would anyone else be around to disrupt your conversation with God if it were *"very early [in the morning]"* in a *"solitary place"*? Even after an exhausting evening of ministry, Yeshua knew the importance of getting alone with God for prayer. Can we afford to do any less?

෫ ෬

ADONAI, wake me up. Get me out of bed and on my knees before You. I praise You, Father, for I am helpless without You. Speak to me, Abba, Father, teach me by Your Spirit. In the morning, I seek Your face. Show me where to go and how to get there, Father. I rely solely on You, my Savior and Shield....

Perseverant Faith

*"All these [people were still living] by faith
[when they] died, not having received the
promises, but having seen them from afar, and
having been persuaded [of them], and having
welcomed them, and having confessed that
they were strangers and sojourners upon the
earth (for those saying such things made it
known that they sought their fatherland). If,
indeed, they had been mindful of that from
which they came forth, they might have had
an opportunity to return, but now they long
for a better [fatherland], that is, a heavenly
[one], where God is not ashamed of them—to
be called their God—for He prepared for them
a city."* עִבְרִים *Iv'riym (Hebrews) 11:13-16*

Av'raham, by faith, had to accept God's promise
that *"[what is] called your 'seed' will be in Yitz'chak."*
(vs. 18) Hevel, 'Chanok, and Noach before him; Ya'akov,
Yosef and Moshe after him—*"all these,"* according to
the letter writer, were still living *"by faith [when they]
died,"* though *"not having received the promises."* These
may have been *"strangers and sojourners upon the earth,"*
but they were no strangers to the bridge that joins the
faithful to the promise: *perseverance.*

Our faith falls short because we give up too easily
when we don't see the promise coming. We look for
signs that the promise is on its way, and we try to gauge
the time frame so that we can pace ourselves. Yet all too

often we wash out, having placed our faith in something that is obviously—at least to our natural minds—not coming to pass.

But Faith asks the question, "Will you keep on trusting God for something you may *never* see?" While our flesh says that "seeing is believing," the promise invites us to stay the course, *despite* what we see. The Spirit of God exhorts us, *"And faith comes from a confidence of things hoped for; a conviction of matters not seen." (vs. 1)*

God is the Keeper of Promises, and by perseverant faith, we believe that we will see all His promises come to pass. But the key is to live our lives as if we will have to *keep* living by faith until we die, seeing and welcoming every promise only from afar. We long for a better fatherland—and God is not ashamed of us *because* of our faith. Therefore, let us be persuaded of the promises… for, indeed, He has prepared for us a city!

෨ ෬

Abba Father, show me how to receive Your promises based on my trust in You alone. Teach me that I can rest on Your promises simply because You made them, and You are the Promise Keeper. Your Word is more than enough for me. Thank You, Lord, for allowing me to receive Your promises, that I will be blessed beyond my understanding. Even when I can't see two feet in front of my face, I will keep running without fear, because You are leading my every step….

To Become Nothing

> "Thus said ADONAI: 'What—have your
> fathers found in Me perversity, That they
> have gone far off from Me, And go after noth-
> ing, and [themselves] become nothing?"
> יִרְמְיָהוּ Yir'm'yahu (Jeremiah) 2:5

We move away from God for various reasons—
sometimes we are ashamed of our own sinfulness, other
times we just simply go our own way. But through the
prophet, ADONAI asks a question that reveals the broken-
heartedness He feels for His people. "Is it me? Am I so
terrible? Did I do something wrong?" It ought to grieve
our hearts to know that we cause the Lord to feel such
rejection by His children.

So, He asks, "Have your fathers found in Me perver-
sity, That they have gone far off from Me...?" This is not
the kind of rejection in which the undesired one is simply ignored. ADONAI is so completely abandoned by His
people that they want to run away from Him—to get as
far from Him as possible. This is the exact *opposite* of
the response the people of God should have toward
their Maker.

To compound the matter, ADONAI is not simply
rejected, He is not just becoming far removed from His
people, but His children are actually moving away from
their Father *in pursuit* of something else—and that
something else is: nothing. ADONAI says, that when the
people of God go "far off from" Him, they are made to

"go after nothing"—and what is worse, they themselves *"become nothing."*

When we reject ADONAI, we ourselves are rejected. Running to embrace a void causes us to become null ourselves. What is there about ADONAI with which we can find fault, that we might justify running away from Him? Is it the brilliant light of holiness that shines continually on our sinful ways? Is it His commands that keep us from straying outside His protective boundaries? How long will we reject a God in whom we can find no wrong? How long will we choose nothing over everything?

൭ ൭

Abba, forgive me for going so far away from You— for going after nothing instead of pursuing You with all that I am. I praise You, ADONAI, for no wrong can be found in You. Teach me to follow Your path and to not stray from it. Help me to never repeat the error of my ancestors' ways. I bless Your name, O God, for You are the One who is highly exalted...

You Don't Know

*"Do not boast about tomorrow, for
you do not know what the day may bring."*
מִשְׁלֵי *Mish'lei (Proverbs) 27:1*

In Yeshua, we can have great confidence in our future. We know that ADONAI will provide for our every need, and we can rest on the promises of God. We can trust and have faith that the Father is leading us, so we may boldly move forward with every confidence. There is no need to worry in Messiah. Indeed, ADONAI has great plans for us—all we need to do is walk the way Yeshua walked, and we will live in victory.

There is a line, however, between confidence and presumptuous faith—and that line is marked by *boasting*. Though we have the mind of Messiah, we are not to *"boast about tomorrow,"* because ultimately, we *"do not know what the day may bring."* Faith gives us confidence to walk forward into the unknown—pre-sumptuous faith takes advantage of trust and imposes our plans on God's. Boasting about tomorrow—even boasting *in the Lord*—can cross a line if we are not careful.

But in the Messianic life, there is another factor to consider: the things God has already revealed to us about tomorrow. Not only do we have confidence that the Father has all things in his hands, but we also have confidence that He can and will show us—and has even shown us already—plans and details *about* the future, so that we may be prepared to follow Him. Yet even though the Lord may have given us a glimpse into the things to come, we still need to evaluate where we are each day. We need to make sure that our eyes are still on Him, and that we are on track with the Father and His plans for us.

This is our challenge—to allow faith to function as it was intended. Faith is day by day, and we cannot hope to have a true faith-walk with ADONAI if we are not getting our instructions from Him on a daily basis. If we are *weak* in the faith and do not stay in constant communication with the Father, we will stray from the path into fear, depression and ineffectiveness. If we are *strong* in faith but don't consult with the Lord, we will grow wild and out of control, presuming to know much more than we really do—soon to have faith only in ourselves.

This is why we ought not to boast about tomorrow: though we may be informed about what to expect, there is only One who truly knows what the day may bring.

❧ ❦

Abba, Father, increase my faith! In every unknowable moment, let me have confidence that You are leading me into Life. Teach me, ADONAI, to be patient—especially when I know what lies ahead—and to walk only along Your perfect path, in Your perfect timing. I bless You, ADONAI, for You never tell me too much, lest I boast about things of which I do not know. Thank You, Lord, for showing me the future—and for not allowing me to go there without You.

Joy, Prayer, Thanks

*"Rejoice always; pray continually; in
everything give thanks, for this is the will of
God in Messiah Yeshua in regard to you."*
1Thessalonians 5:16-18

Easier said than done! Complain always, ignore God
continually, in everything be ungrateful—that's more
like reality, isn't it? It goes against every ounce of our
flesh to give God the attention He deserves. Hence, this
exhortation strikes at the heart of our chronic inability
to get over our circumstances and on with our lives.

Rejoice—always. We are not commanded to always
be *happy*; indeed, "happy" isn't even half-way to joy! He
wants us to be *full*, and more than that, full of *joy*. We
can rejoice that we are able to serve another day, rejoice
that our God loves us, and rejoice that we know the
power of salvation. Joy is deep—it is not shallow at all.
Joy penetrates our dreams and pierces our fears. Joy
captures the light of Messiah and brings revival to our
souls. *"Rejoice always,"* is a command with a promise:
always be joyful, and you will be full of joy… *always!*

Pray—continually. How often is too often to pray?
How regular is too regular to eat of the bread of life and
drink from living waters? How much is too much to
hear the voice of the Creator, our Abba Father? *"Pray
continually"* is far more than petition. It's *conversation*,
periods of speaking and times of listening… it's *relationship*, spending time together and getting to know
each other intimately… it's *fellowship*, revitalizing us,

encouraging us, empowering us, giving us strength wisdom, purpose and direction...

Give thanks—in everything. When you remember? When it's convenient? When things are going well? When He gets us out of a huge mess? *"In everything give thanks"* —in all circumstances, big and small; in joy and despair, whether trivial or monumental. Why? He deserves it. He is ADONAI. Giving thanks *reminds* us that He is God, He guides our steps, protects our way, teaches us, builds our character, and makes us into the disciples of Messiah we are today—and are to become in the future.

Giving thanks in everything, praying continually, rejoicing always—commands, yet commands with blessing. Determine to do these things, and these things will determine your destiny.

༄ ༁

Abba Father, I want to walk and talk and spend time with You. Let me find You in my joy, let me sit at Your hand in prayer, let me bow at Your feet in thanksgiving. Gird up my determination to fight for my fellowship with You, to combat the lethargic spirits that would keep me from praising You. Thank You, ADONAI —You are my everything, and in everything You will have my praise....

Live to Tell

"So speak to them all these words,
but they will not listen to you; and call
to them, but they will not answer you."
יִרְמְיָהוּ *Yir'm'yahu (Jeremiah) 7:27*

The Word of ADONAI through Yir'm'yahu the Prophet
told a tale of destruction—almost utter annihilation for
adulterous Yis'rael. Called from his "childhood," Yir'm'-
yahu was put in the uncomfortable position of having
to prophesy to a nation that was not inclined to listen to
the true prophetic word—he preached the ultimate in
"turn or burn," "fire and brimstone."

Imagine having vision upon vision, receiving word
after word, sitting daily in the counsel of ADONAI receiving His instruction, knowing God's complete, total and
perfect will for your life from a young age. Then, as He
releases you into your ministry, He calls after you, "By
the way, all this that I have called you from the womb to
say to my people Yis'rael—your very life's destiny—will
fall on deaf ears. Even though the entire purpose of your
life is to proclaim My word to My people... *no one is
going to listen to you.* Yes, I have called you to speak, but
no one will hear."

Consider the awesome load of a life that consists of
pouring out to others all day long, yet never receiving
back any form of encouragement or indication that you
are making a positive impact in someone's life. Multiply
that with the factor that no one even listens to a word

you say. Such was the life of Yir'm'yahu the Prophet. What could possibly be the point of such an existence?

Devoting our lives to ADONAI means that we will follow and obey Him regardless of the impact *we* perceive we are having on other peoples' lives. Our success in Messiah cannot be measured by any standard except by our complete submission to do only as ADONAI commands. If we find our value in how many people we lead to salvation, how many people are in our congregations, or how many people we can get to think like we do, we will always end up considering ourselves failures.

Our job is to do as Yir'm'yahu did: *"speak to them."* Speak the truth in love, don't hold back, and don't compromise. Live according to the Word of God, be led by the Spirit, and submit to and obey the Father. That's really all we can do. Even though we *"speak to them,"* they may never listen. And that's okay. It's not our job to make them hear—all we're supposed to do is make the call.

ॐ ◌

ADONAI, I fall on my face before You in worship, and I submit my life only to You. You are the sole assurance I need in order to do as I am told—to speak even if no one will hear. Abba, teach me to expect fruit as a result of my testimony, but show me how to be satisfied with any return that You see fit to yield. I bless Your Name, ADONAI, Chooser of Men for the fulfillment of divine plans. Thank You, Father, for choosing this vessel to be devoted to You alone.

Hold On to Your Way

*"And the righteous holds on to his way,
And the clean of hands grows in strength…"*
איוב *Iyov (Job) 17:9*

One very revealing method for determining the state of our hearts is to watch what we do with our hands. The actions of our hands express our assent or commitment—they indicate the things that we think are important, and the things to which we are willing to bind ourselves. With our hands, we can cut a covenant or cut someone's throat—either way, our actions reveal the condition of our hearts.

Our hands will always be a witness against us, showing where we have been and what we have been doing. The residue of our lives stains our hands each time we dabble in questionable or sinful things. The only way to keep our hands from becoming dirty is to not allow them to participate in even one thing that will leave a mark. Yes, ADONAI can wipe away the filth of our past, but it is only by our cooperation and participation in His holiness that we will be able to keep our hands clean.

"The righteous holds on to his way"—he is able to get a firm grip without interference, because nothing adversely affects his grasp. Depending on our past

involvements, our hands may be so slippery that we can't keep a tight hold on things that are important. Or perhaps our hands are so gummed up and sticky that we cannot let go of things that are worthless—or even harmful—to our walk. Our hands must be clean so that every muscle and fiber will be able to work exactly as they were designed, and we will maintain the integrity of our strength.

"The clean of hands grows in strength"—he doesn't stand still, but moves forward in God's righteousness. As our hands are strengthened, we are able to make easy work of pulling ourselves along the rope of holiness and sanctification. God wants us to do more than just hang on for dear life. He wants us to progress toward the goal—and we can only do so if our hands are clean. The more we hold back from participating in things that will make us unclean, the stronger we will grow… and we will have the integrity to hold on.

ॐ ✍

Abba, Father, make me a servant with clean hands and a pure heart. Teach me the ways of righteousness, O God, that I may submit to and learn of Your holiness. I bless Your Name, for You are Righteousness. Show me how to pursue You with the strength of my hands. You are worthy of praise, Mighty One. Thank You for making me clean, that I may grow stronger in You….

Person of Understanding

"Rebuke makes more of an impression on
the [person of] understanding than a hundred
blows on a fool." מִשְׁלֵי Mish'lei (Proverbs) 17:10

A rebuke can take on many forms. Rebukes can
be subtle, made with only enough emphasis to cause
someone to notice he has a problem. Rebukes can be
direct, yet given with much love and graciousness.
Rebukes can be harsh, made with forceful and con-
frontational communication. But if the principle of
rebuking is correct—no matter what the style of the
rebuke—one factor must be in place for it to make an
impression: the person being rebuked must be a
"[person of] understanding."

So what kind of impression does a rebuke make
on a person *without* understanding? You may as well
pummel him a hundred times—he will never hear you.

A true rebuke is never made out of exasperation,
frustration, anger or resentment. Rebukes come from
love, and a true rebuke will always be loving rather than
abusive. But what do you do when you rebuke someone
in love and it doesn't seem to make an impression?

Nothing.

Once you've made the rebuke, you've done your job. Now it's up to ADONAI, for only He can give understanding. When understanding is not forthcoming in someone you have rebuked, this is not an open invitation to start beating the devil out of them.

Many times, rebukes will go unheeded, for it is our nature to not accept reproof. If we remember that rebukes are for the benefit of the person being rebuked —not to satisfy our own sense of dissatisfaction or irritation with the other person—then we are rebuking with the right spirit, and ADONAI will honor it. So let us be mindful to avoid all self-serving motivation when we approach another with a rebuke. After all, which of us is above correction?

❧ ❧

ADONAI, teach me how to rebuke and be rebuked in a spirit of humility. May I never give correction with impure motives, but help me to truly love others more than myself. I bless You, Abba, for sending people into my life who love me enough to rebuke me, that I may be corrected and put back on the path toward You. Make an impression on me, O God—make me a person of understanding....

Back in the Boat

*"In the fourth watch of the night, Yeshua
came toward them, walking on the sea. The
disciples saw Him walking on the sea, [and]
were terrified. [They] said, 'It is a ghost!' and
they screamed in fear. Immediately, Yeshua
spoke to them, saying, 'Take courage, it is I, do
not be afraid.' And כֵּיפָא, Keifa answered Him,
saying, 'Master, if it is You, command me to
come to You on the water.' [Yeshua] said,
'Come,' and having gone down from the boat,
כֵּיפָא, Keifa walked on the water toward Yeshua.
But seeing the strong wind, [כֵּיפָא, Keifa] was
afraid, and began to sink. He screamed, saying,
'Master, save me!' Immediately, Yeshua stretched
out His hand, caught him, and said to him,
'[Such] little faith! Why did you doubt?' and as
they went into the boat, the wind died down.'"*
מַתִּתְיָהוּ *Matit'yahu (Matthew) 14:25-32*

Was it an act of faith that got Keifa out on that
water? The disciples were screaming with fear at the
sight of this "ghost." When they learned it was Yeshua,
what was Keifa's response? *"If it is you..."* he says, unsure
that his Master indeed stands astern. Is it possible that
Keifa was motivated to get out of the boat and go to
Yeshua, not by *faith*, but by *fear*? Have you ever taken
a "step of faith" because you were just too terrified to
stay where you were?

Full of fear, Keifa stepped onto the water and began
to walk toward Yeshua. As he walked, he noticed what

the wind was pointing out—Keifa was standing on water! Realizing the absurdity of his situation, Keifa panicked and began to sink. The fear that he had brought with him from the boat began to weigh him down. He cried out to the Master, Yeshua took hold of him where he was, and together they went up into the boat. As they did, the revealing wind died down. Keifa, with little faith and much doubt, was right back where he started—the only difference being that now he was all wet.

Walking by *fear* in Yeshua—because we're just too terrified of the alternative—is not life. It's an endless circle of getting out of the boat, then getting back in the boat, never making it all the way across the water. When our faith and trust only go so far, so will we. The Lord does not take us further than we are able to go on our own—so when we step out of the boat, it can't start with fear, or we will surely sink. Thankfully, He will always save us and get us back into the boat. But what He really wants is for us to walk on water, and the only way we can do that is to truly cast our cares into the sea....

છ્ન ન્ક

Abba, Father, increase my faith today. Help me to unstrap myself from the cares of my burdens and to walk in trust. I bless You, ADONAI, for You will always save me when I call. I praise You, Abba, because You are teaching me to not spend my life calling, but *coming* when *You* call for *me*. Thank You, God, for Your graciousness and patience. Let Your peace abound in my heart....

An Opening of Eyes

"The Spirit of יְהוָה אֲדֹנָי, *Adonai* ELOHIYM
is *on me, because* ADONAI *has anointed me to
proclaim good news to the humble. He sent me
to bind the broken of heart, to proclaim liberty
to captives, and an opening [of eyes] to ones
[that are] bound; to proclaim the year of the
good pleasure of* ADONAI, *and the Day of vengeance of our God; to comfort all mourners; to
give [comfort] to [those who] mourn in Zion;
to bestow to them garlands instead of ashes, the
oil of joy instead of mourning, a garment of
praise for a spirit of weakness. And He is calling to them, 'Oaks of Righteousness, the Planting of* ADONAI'—*[that He may] be glorified.'"*
יְשַׁעְיָהוּ *Y'sha'yahu (Isaiah) 61:1-3*

A life in Messiah is one that is turned on its head.
What was formerly *up* is now *down*; what was *north* is
now *south*; what was *right* is now *wrong*. Our reality
before we knew Messiah was one of deception and false
images—what we perceived as light was merely a dim
glow; what we saw as beautiful was really plain… and
what we called "gray" was truly the pit of darkness.
Messiah came to lift the veil from our eyes that we
might see our physical reality through the enhanced
vision of the Spirit.

Once we are turned right-side up in Messiah, we
begin a process of shedding our former ways and
thoughts, since spiritual gravity is finally at our feet.

As we lose the old things, the new man—the new creation we have become in Messiah—receives genuine replacements for the counterfeits we were once forced to keep.

Garlands instead of ashes... life for death. *Joy instead of mourning*... light for darkness. *A garment of praise for a spirit of weakness*... a breakthrough of thanksgiving for the weight of our own burdens. We exchange the reality our sin had brought upon us for the reality in Messiah. We are now righteous, new creations born from above —the old man is gone, the new man has come!

This is our freedom: we need no longer be poor in spirit, for we are rich in praise; we are no longer bound and captive, but have been released from the prison of our former selves. ADONAI takes pride in His new creation —we cannot, then, hide the great work he has done in us under the cloud of a heavy spirit, behind the face of a mourner, covered in ashes.

In Messiah, we are planted, mighty *Oaks of Righteousness*... free from oppression, and comforted by the One who makes us righteous.

 తా౼ ౼ం

ADONAI, show me that I no longer need to continue to wear the clothes of a sinner. Teach me that I am no longer dressed as one ashamed. Let me realize that I am righteous by Your hand—a new creation by Your Holy Spirit. Thank You, Father, for turning my life right-side up and exchanging my old self for the new. Clothe me in praise, ADONAI! Cover me in joy, my God! Lift the spirit of weakness, O Lord! I praise You, Adonai ELOHIYM, that You may be glorified!

*"Come, hear, all you who fear God, and
I [will] recount what He did for my soul. To
Him with my mouth I call, and exaltation is
under my tongue. [But] iniquity, if I see [it] in
my heart, ADONAI will not hear. But God has
heard, He has attended to the voice of my
prayer. Blessed is God, Who has not turned
aside my prayer, and His loving-kindness,
from me!"* תְּהִלִּם *T'hillim (Psalms) 66:16-20*

With our mouths, we cry out to the Lord; with
our tongues, we offer praise. As we lift up petition and
prayer to our Maker, we do so with the expectation that
we will be heard and our prayers will be answered. But
with all the words of adoration and praise, we may as
well be spitting curses if we are attempting to keep our
sins hidden within us.

We can praise God with our voices and bless the
name of ADONAI with our lips, we can get the prayer
exactly right and say all the correct words—yet He is
within *His* right to reject our prayers and turn his grace
away. How can this be? ADONAI will not listen to us if
we hold iniquity in our hearts.

It is one thing to have sinful temptations, and yet
another for evil thoughts to creep in and cause us to

stumble. But to see iniquity in our hearts is to embrace it, love it, caress it—to stroke and fondle it with care. We are given over to evil thoughts when we entertain them at length, fantasize about them, protect them, and keep godly thoughts from intruding upon them.

All the praise we can muster, all the blessings we bestow—they will be ignored if we see and hold onto the iniquity in our hearts. No amount of perfectly placed words or Scriptural sentiments can manipulate ADONAI into overlooking the true love of our hearts. If we cherish anything in our hearts and minds above Him, we are truly without fear. God will not listen; He will surely turn away. But if our blessings and praise come from a heart that cherishes ADONAI, He will pay attention to our prayers—and we will be able to boast in Him and *"recount what He did for my soul..."*

⁎ ⁎

ADONAI, give me a pure heart that is devoted only to You. Abba, may I not entertain evil thoughts and allow them to captivate my mind, keeping me from thinking only of You. Father, I *do* bless Your name, and I praise You. Thank You, Master, for paying attention to my prayers. Blessed be You, ADONAI, who does not reject my prayer or turn His loving-kindness away from me...

Weights and Measures

"All the ways of a man are pure in his own eyes, And ADONAI weighs the spirit."
מִשְׁלֵי *Mish'lei (Proverbs) 16:2*

We live in a relative-thinking world. Even in the Body of Messiah, there is little agreement on what, if anything, is *absolute*. When we ask ourselves, "What would Yeshua do?" this is really a question of absolutes. The question presupposes—though we may not realize it—that in every situation there is an exact, *godly* way to respond and an exact, *ungodly* way to respond. ADONAI deals in absolutes. Though they may not always make sense to us—and we may not even agree—His determination of right and wrong is the only one that matters.

"All the ways of a man are pure in his own eyes..." We are designed to be thinkers, for we are made in the image of God. It is in our nature to believe fully in whatever we think. Our minds tell us that if we are capable of thinking something, then it must be true—it must be good, and right, and *absolute*. But the fact that we are able to conjure up an idea in our own minds doesn't mean that it is true, much less the *only* truth.

ADONAI gave us the ability to think for ourselves, but He has also given us the standard for self-appraisal: The

Scriptures—and Yeshua, the living Word. Indeed, it is to our benefit to assess the standard first, before we try things out on our own. We are bound to get haughty and caught up in our own relativity if we are initially unaware of God's absoluteness.

ADONAI weighs our spirit by putting us in one hand and Yeshua in the other—and most often, our side of the scale is much heavier than His. We are weighed down with egotism, self-reliance, haughtiness, judgmentalism, and a condescending nature. But living only according to the Scriptures is not a burdensome lifestyle as some may think. Indeed, it keeps the weight off our shoulders and makes our burden light—there are no negative by-products of our own self to weigh us down. Our spirit is light when we look to Yeshua as the sole standard of weights and measures, because He enables us to say "Yes!" to the absolutes and "No!" to all the extra weight.

∂∾ ∞

Yeshua, nothing is pure but You—no one is pure but You. Help me to see the impurity of my own ways, and teach me to walk in the holiness of Your absoluteness. Show me the error in my relative thinking; reveal to me that I am not the center of my world, but You are the One I am to center *myself* around. ADONAI, weigh my spirit, and let it be one like that of Messiah—free me from the weight of my own thoughts that are holding me down. Release me, Master, that I may be empowered to walk according to Your ways....

I Want to Know You

"And it came to pass in their discussing and reasoning together, that Yeshua himself, having come near, walked along with them, and their eyes were kept so as not to recognize Him..." Luke 24:15-16

What is it that keeps us from recognizing the Master when we are in His presence? Indeed, what keeps us from even recognizing that we are in His presence at all? Have we merely forgotten His promises, or did we never really believe them in the first place?

Does ADONAI truly guide us and protect us, giving us power and an abundant life—or do we just think it would be nice if He did? Has God moved in our lives in such a mysterious, miraculous way that we know without doubt that He sovereignly works on our behalf—or do we just think it would be nice if He did? Was Yeshua really resurrected from the dead, defeating death and satisfying God's justice so that we would receive eternal life and forgiveness for our sins—or do we just think it would have been nice if He had?

God moves, whether we know it or not. ADONAI comes close to us, whether we see Him or not. Recognizing the Master is no more and no less than simply seeing—not just seeing with our eyes, but with our inner being.

Did you wake up this morning? God is near. Did you take your first breath today? God is near. Can you lift your eyes to Heaven and praise His holy Name? *God is near.*

What kind of proof does the Master need to offer? Do we need a burning bush? A voice from Heaven? A simple healing miracle, perhaps? Maybe some prophetic foresight about the future?... Does ADONAI need to perform some confounding feat in order for us to know He is here? That's what the world expects. The world is accustomed to smoke and mirrors, and if something happens to be "unexplainable," then perhaps it can be attributed to "God." But we have the ultimate proof... irrefutable proof... we *know* Him. We recognize Him because we *know* Him.

We've heard His voice, seen His face, touched His glory, smelled His sweetness, tasted His goodness—this is not some invisible, unrecognizable god. We recognize Him because we *know* Him, and we *know* Him because He is real... and alive!

❧ ❧

ADONAI, show me Your face; remind me again of how real You truly are. Teach me to recognize You when You're standing right in front of me. Let me touch You and embrace You—do not be a shadow to me any longer, but let me see You and hear You. Let me know You so that I will never miss a chance to be in Your presence... to walk with You, and talk with You... to come near...

That No One Takes You Captive

"*See that no one takes you captive through philosophy and empty deception, according to the [teachings] delivered by men, [or] according to the elements of the cosmos, and not according to Messiah.*" Colossians 2:8

There is nothing wackier than the ideas human beings come up with at times. We can really dream up some whoppers, given the chance. We have this ability because the Creator has bestowed upon us an incredible potential for creativity. Unfortunately, we far too easily give ourselves credit for the amazing things we can conceive in our minds. This causes us to take pride in the things we think—much more than we ought.

Philosophy is an interesting word. It means, "love of wisdom." This is not the same kind of "love of wisdom" that the Scriptures encourage—no, "wisdom" in the Scriptures is that which comes from ADONAI. "Philosophy" is love for our own intellectual pursuits and our own ideas, which are set *against* the wisdom of ADONAI. We are warned against being taken "*captive through philosophy*" because it is an "*empty deception*" —by its very design, it draws us away and imprisons us in our own minds.

One thing you will never see is a lonely philosopher —he will always have at least a handful of disciples. The wisdom of men seeks out impressionable minds because it needs to breed to stay alive. This is antagonistic toward the Spirit of Messiah, the rightful owner of men's minds. The spirit of philosophy leads us to consider *"the [teachings] delivered by men"* and *"the elements of the cosmos"* as legitimate fountains of knowledge and truth. But in the end, they are nothing but empty deceptions.

Love of wisdom and pursuit of intellect will draw us away from the truth. We are not to be taken captive by the philosophies of men or the mysteries of the universe, but we are to walk in the teachings that are *"according to Messiah."* In Yeshua, we have a trustworthy source of wisdom and knowledge, and a Teacher who deserves our allegiance as disciples. As we run from the intellectual pursuits of men, may we be captivated by the Messiah— in whom we have the peace of knowing that we are truly free.

಄ ಄

Master, I praise You—shield my mind from the deceptive philosophies of the world. Show me how to keep from falling into the trap of intellectual pursuits, that I may pursue You and Your ways alone. ADONAI, I bless Your Name, for You have given me a mind that seeks to understand You. Show me Your ways, O Lord, and teach me the true ways of wisdom, which I love....

Eeeew!

"'[And you, son of man, make bread.] You will eat it—a barley-cake. And with excrement—the filth of [a] man—you will bake it before [Yis'rael's] eyes...' And I said, 'Oh! אֲדֹנָי יהוה*, Adonai ELOHIYM, behold, my soul has never [been] defiled. No carcass or thing torn [by wild animals] have I eaten, from my youth even until now, nor has abominable flesh come into my mouth!' And He said to me, '[Very well.] See, I will give to you cow manure instead of man's excrement, and you will make your bread upon it.'"* יְחֶזְקֵאל *Y'chez'ke-el (Ezekiel) 4:12-15*

How would you respond if ADONAI told you to draw a picture of Jerusalem and wage a miniature-scale war against it, complete with little, tiny battering rams and terrain? What would you do if He then instructed you to lie down on your left side in front of the picture in order to lay siege against it—and what if He told you to do this every day for more than a full year? What if, after the year was up, He simply told you to flip over and do it again on your right side—but this time you could stop after just six weeks? What if this was a fairly accurate synopsis of the vision that ADONAI gave to Y'chez'ke-el in the first half of chapter four?

And what if ADONAI then instructed you to make bread? Not just any bread made from wheat and barley, and prepared in an ordinary manner—no, this bread is to be cooked in a *very* special way. What would you do, if ADONAI told you to make the bread by baking it over a nice, hot, steamy pile of flaming human excrement? Of course, you'd think to yourself, "Nothing strange or disgusting about that! I hear, and I obey," right? Or perhaps you would do what Y'chez'ke-el did, bringing the unfolding vision to a screeching halt with your spontaneous outburst of shock and dismay. *"Behold, my soul has never [been] defiled!"* So what if the Creator of the universe actually conceded to you, saying you didn't have to use human excrement to bake your bread after all? What if, in His concession, He said you were free to use cow manure instead?

Would you do it?

There would be something really wrong with us if we thought there was nothing strange about what ADONAI commanded Y'chez'ke-el in his vision. But there would also be something really wrong with us as disciples of Messiah if we refused to wholeheartedly follow and obey just because His instructions made us uncomfortable. We have to be honest with ourselves and make a decision: are we only willing to walk with Messiah as long as we don't have to get our hands dirty, or are we going to obey according to whatever manner we're called—even if it means getting soiled every now and then? So ask yourself, "How am I going to make my bread? Will it be according to my recipe or His?"

∞ ∞

ADONAI, sometimes I don't understand how You can say such things, but teach me to follow and obey in spite of my ignorance. I praise You, O Holy One, for even defilement can bring cleansing if it is commanded in Your Word. I bless You, ADONAI, for the way You catch me off guard and teach me Your truth… even in the most unusual ways…

Inside My House

"I [will] act wisely [and follow] a path of
integrity; when will you come to me? I [will]
walk habitually in the integrity of my heart,
inside my house." תְהִלִּם T'hillim (Psalms) 101:2

One of the most important standards set for us
in Scripture is the standard of integrity. Usually, the
concept of integrity is wrapped up in the idea of moral
or ethical behavior. But what if integrity is more than
just the measure of how we *act*, and is instead a reflection of who we truly are at the core of our being?

We are taught that there is a path called "integrity."
Some might think this a slender, winding path—difficult to find and shrouded in shrubbery and foliage. Others
may believe it is a hearty, straight path that cuts through
the underbrush—easy to see and simple to follow. Yet it
seems that the ability to walk the path of integrity does not
have to do with the path itself, but with how *we* choose
to walk it. Although the path is indeed straight and clear,
only the one who is upright can follow it—the one who
lets his eyes stray to the left or the right will go his own
way.

This path is not far from us. In fact, it begins inside
our own house. If we treat our spouses poorly and with
contempt, who will see? If we indulge our fantasies and
desires behind closed doors, who can witness it? Integrity
is not just what other people see—indeed, we can mas-
querade and allow people to see only what we choose.
Integrity is walking righteously because we *are* the

righteousness of Messiah. The One who sees us even in secret does not only see our righteous acts, but our sincere heart of integrity.

When we follow the path of integrity, it is with proper expectation—that as we walk the path, ADONAI will come to us. It is only along this one path that He can be found. When we give in to our emotions, our perceptions or our biases, we will no doubt be led astray. To stay on the path, we must set aside our own need for control and walk *habitually* in integrity—submitted to God, yielded to the Spirit, and living according to His Word. When will He come to me? When I walk the one path and no other...

৵ ৶

ADONAI, make me a person of integrity. Teach me that integrity is not something I do, but something I am. Show me Your ways, ADONAI, that I may be quick to recognize areas of compromise in my life—places with a breach in integrity. I praise You, O God, for You are perfect and holy in everything. Help me to pursue You in that holiness, that I may follow the path of righteousness and walk only in Your ways.

Good News 101

*"And I make known to you, brothers, the
Good News that I proclaimed to you, which
you also received, in which also you have stood,
through which you also are being saved if you
hold fast in what words I proclaimed Good
News to you—otherwise you have believed in
vain..." 1Corinthians 15:1*

In the Messianic community of Corinth, some of
the believers were waffling on the issue of resurrection.
They were going so far as to say that there is no resurrection from the dead—which, of course, would preclude
Yeshua's own resurrection. Paul points out that if Yeshua
is not resurrected, then the entirety of the Good News is
nullified.

*"Messiah died for our sins, according to the Scriptures,
and that He was buried, and that He rose on the third day,
according to the Scriptures..."* (vs. 3) When we forget,
ignore, or dismiss the fundamentals of the faith, we
abolish the Good News and make it completely void of
power. Knowing the foundation of the Good News is as
important to our walk as simple, childlike belief. Without
the Good News of the Messiah Yeshua, we are a lost cause.

Having a solid, foundational understanding of the
Good News is key to our salvation. Indeed, Paul shows
how the Good News is crucial to every stage of our
spiritual growth. First, we receive it—like an infant at
his mother's breast, the Good News nourishes us as we
grow, gain our balance and begin to walk. Then we stand

—as maturing believers, the Good News is the only foundation upon which our spiritual lives can be built. Finally, we are being saved—if we hold fast to the Good News, it will finish its work and we will see our ultimate salvation.

The key is to remember the *condition* placed on our walk and our salvation: we will receive, take our stand, and be saved *only if* we *keep holding fast* to that same Good News. In other words, the Good News is our ultimate provision and the only assurance of our salvation. If we refuse our provision, we lose our assurances—that's the nature of the Good News.

Believing a different version of the Good News—or even a *partial* version—is all in vain... it does not have the power to save. It all comes down to the work Yeshua did when He hung on the Tree, and what happened next, on the third day. Yeshua is alive, having died for our sins and been raised from the dead. But don't forget—receive it, stand on it, and keep holding... fast.

‎و۔ ۔‎

Yeshua, You are my provision; Father, my provider. Abba, thank You for resurrecting Your Son who died for my sins—this is the nourishing milk I receive, the grace by which I stand, and the gift by which I am being saved. Teach me to keep holding fast to Your Good News, and to remember Your provision. Thank You, Father... You have all my love and devotion, which I give to You as a sacrifice of praise....

The Punishment of Love

*"And it will come to pass, when [the people]
say, 'Why has ADONAI our God done all these
[things] to us?' that you are to say to them,
'[Just] as you have abandoned Me and served
the gods of a foreigner in your land, so [likewise]
will you serve strangers in a land [that is] not
yours.'"* יִרְמְיָהוּ *Yir'm'yahu (Jeremiah) 5:19*

Does ADONAI punish His people? Yes, he does. Does
a father punish his child? Yes, he does. It does not mean
that the father no longer *loves* his child—on the contrary;
he would be displaying his hatred if he stood by and did
nothing as his son went his own way. Punishment that is
not vindictive, malicious or spiteful can often be the very
definition of love in action. And so, ADONAI punishes
His people when they go their own way—it's all part of
the Promise.

A poor father, however, will punish his child like this:
"Just as you abandoned me and loved another father, so
likewise I will abandon you and love another child." That's
punishment, all right. But it's also malevolent and down-
right mean. This isn't a father—it's a big baby. "If you
don't like me, then I won't like you..." He is not showing
love for his child—he is being hurtful and cruel.

Yet isn't this what we expect to read when ADONAI
says, *"[Just] as you have abandoned Me and served the*

gods of a foreigner in your land"? Don't we think He will continue by saying, "so likewise I will abandon you, displace you from your land, and love another instead"? But instead, we see true love—punishment that fits the offense. Since Yis'rael abandoned ADONAI and served strange gods in her own land, ADONAI says, "*so [likewise] will you serve strangers in a land [that is] not yours.*" ADONAI does not take away his love and fatherhood, but He does give Yis'rael her due. If she will not serve ADONAI, she will serve *strangers*. If she chooses to defile the land, she will have to do it *somewhere else.*

Even when we abandon Him and take ourselves out from under His protection, He does not abandon us— but He will allow us to walk into prisons of our own making. The good news is that even though we may choose to abandon Him, He will always remain steadfast and true to His word. How thankful we should be that our God is not willing to sit idly by and watch us wander aimlessly through life—instead, He calls us, chooses us and *commits to chastening us* when we go the wrong way.

And, yes, it does hurt Him more than it hurts us....

∂๑ ๑๖

ADONAI, I bless You, Maker and Keeper of promises. Teach me to be quick to respond to Your voice and Your times of discipline, that I may never stray so far as to endure what I deserve. Thank You, Father, for giving me everything I need to follow You and Your ways. You are worthy of praise, ADONAI, disciplinarian of Your children, lover of our souls...

Two Are Better Than One

"*Two* are *better than one, in that they have a good return for their labor, for if they fall, the one raises up his companion. But woe to the one who falls and there is not second [person] to raise him up! Also, if two lie down, then [together] they have heat, but how can one [alone have] heat? And though the one [may be] overpowered [by an attacker], two [can] stand against him; and the threefold cord will not quickly be broken." קֹהֶלֶת Kohelet (Ecclesiastes) 4:9-12*

"The partnership" is a lost form of relationship in today's society. We tend to have neither the trust nor the patience needed to forge a lasting partnership with another human being—resulting in much heartache, breaking of relationships, and eventually, solitude. The partnership is the strongest form of relationship that exists, but if it is not properly grounded in godliness, it will tear apart and be irreparably damaged.

It is no wonder that so many in the Body of Messiah choose individualism over partnership: whenever we change our mind, we don't have to worry about whether another person will agree with us; whenever we break our vows, we don't have to wonder if someone is going to call us on the carpet. In individualism, we can do whatever we want, whenever we want, without concern for the consequences of our actions—especially conflict and confrontation.

But individualists give up more than they gain—indeed, what is to be gained in a life without accountability and aid? Individuals give up the protection, provision, and prosperity that can be found in a true partnership. *"…woe to the one who falls and there is not second [person] to raise him up!"*

The most common type of partnership today is the "Pair of Individuals." You may know some of these partnerships by their modern, alternative name—"the marriage." A husband and wife should be the ultimate partners, yet we see multitudes of failed marriages—and many others that leave much to be desired. Why? Because instead of having a true partnership, the married couple usually attempts to cohabitate as a "pair of individuals"—equal, but separate.

True partnership is not about equality—it is about complementing one another. In true partnership, you know each other's strengths and weaknesses, and you learn to trust and continually rely upon each other. Pride is overcome by humility and love. A *true* partner cares more about the welfare of the other, while trusting that his partner feels exactly the same way.…

᪥ ᪥

Abba, Father, who will lift me up when I fall? Have I even *let* anyone else into my life who would *notice* if I did? Lord, show me where I have been a poor partner, and teach me how to be the kind of person in whom another can place his trust. Bring me out of my individuality, Lord, for two are truly better than one.…

To Him Who Leaves

> *"Discipline is grievous to him who*
> *leaves the way; he who hates reproof dies."*
> מִשְׁלֵי *Mish'lei (Proverbs) 15:10*

"The way" is the path that leads to life. It is the road of salvation, the route to ADONAI. The Scriptures speak of this Way many times in many forms, and in each instance the teaching is clear: though the path is straight and true, a person can leave it at any time—but he will suffer the consequences. The lures of this world cause a man to look aside and be drawn away from the path of righteousness. When this happens, *"discipline is grievous."*

What happens in our minds to make us think that something better or more interesting may be found anywhere but on the Way? Surely, it is because our flesh craves that which it ought not to have. But not soon after going astray, we realize we are in torment and we think, "If I can just get back to the way, everything will be made right." To return to the path, however, one has to endure the fire.

"Discipline is grievous to him who leaves the way; he who hates reproof dies." No matter how easy it was to leave the way, no matter how short a distance we have gone, the only way back is through a consuming fire that will purify our hearts and minds, enabling us to reach the path once again. This is correction and discipline— and without it, we will not live. The fire will not destroy us, for it only removes that which needs to be burned

up. No, death comes when one *"hates reproof"*—when he remains in darkness instead of returning to the path.

Here is the good news: those who have left the way and withstood the correction and discipline of restoration are not so inclined to leave the path again. Purged are the cravings to follow after one's own lusts and desires —replaced by a burning passion for the Holy One and all of His ways. Discipline may be grievous, but it only lasts for a time. If we can endure it, we will be cleansed and made ready to dwell with the One at the end of the Way....

የ ﷼

Abba, Father, I accept Your discipline and correction. Restore me, Abba, that I may delight in the way of Your holiness and righteousness—the way of Your Son. Forgive me, Father, for leaving the path and taking my eyes off of You. I praise You, ADONAI, for You are full of grace and forgiveness—and even now, I am on my way home once again ....

Seeing Is Deceiving

*"As Yeshua went on from there, two blind
men followed him, calling and saying, 'Take
pity on us, Son of David!'"* מַתִּתְיָהוּ *Matit'yahu
(Matthew) 9:27*

Two blind men began following Yeshua. But how
could they follow if they were *blind*? Indeed, *why* would
they follow Him? What miracles had they *seen*? What
great wonders had they *witnessed*? Yet according to
Matit'yahu, these two were the first to recognize that
He was the *"Son of David"*—He was *Messiah!*

Let us put ourselves in the sandals of these two men
for a moment. Probably blind from birth, we had been
outcasts all our life. We made our way through the streets
of N'tzaret by memorizing the roads, our walking sticks
clicking and clacking before us trying to judge the distance
between potential obstacles. Our friends were other
afflicted souls, blind men and beggars. Though we were
Israelites, we were on the outskirts of society—barely
noticed, yet noticing everything.

Then one day we hear of this Yeshua, a miracle-
worker. Could He be the One?

Following the sounds of the crowds, we make our
way to the shores of Lake Kineret, as one of our acquaint-
ances, a paralyzed man, is brought before this one named
Yeshua. After an exchange of words with some of the
local Torah-teachers, the crowd erupts with amazement
and praise to ADONAI! "What has happened?" we cry out

to anyone who will listen. Hardly noticing us, someone shouts back, "The paralyzed man walks! Yeshua has healed him!" Our heart leaps, and in that moment, we know... *Mashiyach has come!* As the crowd rushes off, we are swept along with them, following Yeshua from miracle to miracle, hearing the words of Torah espoused from His lips, and becoming further convinced that He is the One.

The two blind men following Yeshua could not rely on their eyesight for anything, yet all their senses testified that they were in the midst of the One—the Great Deliverer of Yis'rael. How often do we ignore what our senses are plainly telling us? Sometimes our faith can be so one-dimensional that we are unable to see the truth even when it is standing right before us.

Inasmuch as a blind man can follow the Messiah, perhaps we would do well to occasionally close our eyes... and see what we can see....

ॐ ॐ

Abba, Father, open my spiritual eyes that I may see the reality of You. Teach me, Father, to be discerning— to not allow my senses to deceive me, but to let Your Spirit guide me into all truth. I praise You, Yeshua, for You are so great and mighty that even a blind man can see that You are Messiah. Thank You for showing me Your truth—for allowing me to see You, even when my eyes are telling me that You're not there. I bless You, ADONAI, restorer of sight to the blind....

Foreign Wives, Foreign Gods

"And king שְׁלֹמֹה, Sh'lomoh loved many foreign women… of the nations which ADONAI said to the sons of יִשְׂרָאֵל, Yis'rael, 'Do not go among them, and do not [let them] go among you; surely they [will] turn aside your heart after their gods;' [but] שְׁלֹמֹה, Sh'lomoh cleaved to them for love. And it came to pass, at the time of the old age of שְׁלֹמֹה, Sh'lomoh, [that] his wives turned aside his heart after other gods… And ADONAI was angry with שְׁלֹמֹה, Sh'lomoh, for his heart had turned aside from ADONAI, God of יִשְׂרָאֵל, Yis'rael, who had appeared to him twice, and given a charge to him concerning this thing… and ADONAI said to שְׁלֹמֹה, Sh'lomoh, 'Because you have done this… I [will] surely tear the kingdom from you…'" מְלָכִים א M'lachiym Alef (1Kings) 11:1-11

King Sh'lomoh—son of David, heir to the throne of Yis'rael, the wisest and richest man who has ever lived. Yet for all his wealth, wisdom, and accomplishments for ADONAI, Sh'lomoh was an adulterer far worse than his father—he was an adulterer against God.

ADONAI appeared to Sh'lomoh—twice—to warn him of his coming infidelity, and yet he still "cleaved to… many *foreign women... for love...*" By uniting with these women from foreign nations, he turned aside from fully following ADONAI—from being wholehearted toward God. Through his *physical relations* with foreign wives, Sh'lomoh opened himself up to *spiritual relations* with foreign gods.

What was Sh'lomoh's fundamental sin? Loving his wives more than God? Building the high places? Allowing the sacrifices and offerings to strange gods? Sh'lomoh's sin hits at the very root of our faith—indeed, it is the sin that forms the foundation for all other sins.... Sh'lomoh *disobeyed* God. In his disobedience, he allowed his heart to be turned from ADONAI, and the word of the Lord spoken directly to him—*in person*—became meaningless. Sh'lomoh violated one of the most essential commands of Torah: *"You shall have no other gods before me."*

We may not always hear the audible voice of ADONAI, we may not get visits from Him when He has something important to tell us, but we still know what we should and shouldn't do. Foreign wives lead us to foreign gods. Those to whom we cleave in the *physical* will directly affect to whom we cleave in the *spiritual*. So let us turn our hearts to ADONAI, and cleave only to *Him* for love...

&ะ ๛

Father, hold back Your wrath from me and forgive, though I have been an adulterer to You. I have loved others more than I have loved You—and worse, I have disobeyed Your Word. Teach me to forsake all that keeps me from wholehearted devotion to You, my God. I praise You, ADONAI, for You joyfully receive me when I turn from my sin. Thank You, Father, for showing me the way back to You...

A Puff of Air

"He who planted the ear, does He not hear? He who formed the eye, does He not see? He who disciplines the nations, does He not reprove? He who teaches man knowledge is ADONAI. *He knows the thoughts of man, that they* are *a puff of air."* תְּהִלִּם *T'hillim (Psalms) 94:9-11*

How much we know, we mortal thinkers! How intelligent we are, able to unravel the mysteries of God! How spiritual we must be, having the ability to dissect, label and categorize all the aspects of our Creator! How clever we are, thinking that ADONAI cannot see what we are trying to hide.

I remember when my oldest son was three years old, and we would play 'Hide and Seek.' In fact, he was the best 'Hide and Seek' player that has ever lived! He was so amazing that all he had to do was lay on the floor behind a chair and cover his eyes… and *no one* could find him!

The vanity of man is the belief that if *we* aren't looking at *God*, then *He* must not be able to see *us*. We think we can be pious by day, displaying our vast knowledge of the Scriptures or our deep yielding to the Spirit—but at any time, we can simply draw the blinds, close our doors, and we will be in a world that is impenetrable to the eyes of God.

But, the psalmist asks, *"He who planted the ear, does He not hear? He who formed the eye, does He not see?* It is folly to think He doesn't. Yes, the One who teaches man knowledge—He knows it all. You think He's not watching? Think again. Indeed, He fully knows *"the thoughts of man...."*

We think we're so smart in our crafty ways. But all of our thoughts are as brief and without substance as a *"puff of air."* They last but a moment, and then they are gone. There is no evidence of their existence; they make no impact on the world around us. What we *think* is nothing—especially when we think God can't see.

Our thoughts are merely *"a puff of air."* Thankfully, ADONAI is aware of this, and *"He who teaches man knowledge"* has in mind for us a better way....

న్ ∽

ADONAI, open my eyes, that I may see You clearly. Teach me to understand that You know all my ways, and there is nothing I can hide from You. Reveal my ways, O God, and teach me Your knowledge. I praise You, ADONAI, for even Your foolishness is beyond all my understanding. You are worthy of all blessings, Planter of ears, Former of eyes....

There Is No Response

"A slave is not disciplined by words;
though he understands, there is no response."
מִשְׁלֵי *Mish'lei (Proverbs) 29:19*

We are a society of many words, but little action.

How many copies of the Scriptures are on your bookshelf? One? Three? Five? Now, how many books *about* the Scriptures—about the Faith—do you own? Seventeen? Twenty-eight? Forty-two? Indeed! Here you are, reading this devotional—yet another man's "many words" about the Scriptures. How did we get here?

Why is it that hundreds of new faith-related books are published every year? Is it because the Father is revealing so many new and exciting things to His people in this day? Unlikely. It is much more probable that hundreds of authors are teaching the same fundamental truths *over* and *over*, with a different slant or perspective each time. Do they do this because they are trying to make a buck? Not necessarily. It's because even though we, the readers, *understand* the fundamental truths of the Scriptures, *"there is no response."*

"A slave is not disciplined by words…" Why not? Because he is not free. All the words in the world cannot

discipline the slave, because even *"though he understands, there is no response."*

Here is the sad news: though we have been set free in Yeshua, many of us continue to live our lives as slaves to our old ways. We keep going around in circles, struggling with the same areas of flesh, committing old sins, maintaining old habits and attitudes. We read some books, listen to a few messages, and we *understand*... but we don't *respond*.

Does this mean that we need to be beaten like a slave before we will respond to the Word of God? Perhaps if *we* begin to take action, we will find that we are not so slothful after all. Our slave mentality will be thrown off, and we will embrace our true freedom in Messiah.

Listen today, not to the many words of a man, but to the *simple* words of the Father. Understand them, and then *do* them. Respond to the Word—not just in silent agreement, but by allowing it to change your life. Remember the actions of Messiah, comprehend what He did on our behalf... and then *respond*.

‏ 🙢 🙠

Father, I confess—I have been a consumer, rather than a doer of Your Word. I have wanted to be spoon-fed, and I haven't acted on what I know. Forgive me, Lord, and change me. Teach me to be an active disciple —effective for Your kingdom. I praise You, ADONAI, for You have never failed to act on my behalf. I bless Your Name, for you have truly set me free—that I may be enslaved only to You. Teach me, ADONAI, and help me to respond....

A Worse Hole

"No one sews a patch of unshrunk cloth on an old garment, otherwise the new piece will pull up from the old and the tear will become worse. And no one puts new wine into old skins, otherwise, the new wine will burst the skins, and the wine will pour out, and the skins will be destroyed. Indeed, new wine is to be put into new skins." Mark 2:21-22

Pushing a working car. Swimming in your winter coat. Fasting at a wedding feast. What do all these things have in common? They are ridiculous situations. Yet many in the Body of Messiah are trapped in such ludicrousness, unable to escape into sanity. The Master is trying to teach us to see absurdity for what it truly is, and to stop accepting it as reality.

Our old ways as sinners are completely incompatible with our new life in Messiah. What happens when these two worlds—the old and new—collide? Chaos… a fundamental breakdown in our ability to function. Like the new patch tearing away from the old cloth, it leaves a bigger and more irreparable hole than before. When we spend our time trying to simply repair and mend our old life—rather than throwing it away and living in the new—we will only end up as tattered rags.

This is the ridiculous, the absurd, the ludicrous. Again, it is like pouring new wine into old wineskins. One might as well pour it out onto the ground. The Master is telling us to take not only the new wine, but the new *skin* as well! We are given the choice, but the problem is that we really *like* our old, comfortable skin —it suits us, we think. Surely, if we fill ourselves with new wine, it will be sufficient. And what happens? We leak, and then we break.

The Master wants us to take a good, hard look at ourselves and do some housecleaning. It's time to make a move. How much of your old stuff is going to make it onto the truck, and how much is going into the dumpster? We need to remember that even though we might be allowed to take it with us, that doesn't necessarily mean we should. He is giving us a new home with all new furnishings. Bringing our old junk along just doesn't make sense—it belongs in the trash, once and for all....

ﭼ ﯙ

Father, teach me to live in the new life You have given to me. Convince me that I no longer have to live like the person I used to be, but that I am totally new in You! I praise You for saving me, Father, I thank You for giving me life. Open my eyes, that I may distinguish between the absurd and the sane. You are worthy of glory and honor, ADONAI, for You reveal the truth to those who seek it....

Stand

"Put on the whole armor of God, so that you [will] be able to stand against the methods of the Accuser. For we wrestle not with blood and flesh, but with the principalities, with the authorities, with the world-rulers of the darkness of this age, [and] with the spiritual things of evil in the heavenly places. Because of this, take up the whole armor of God, that you may be able to resist in the day of evil, and [after] having done all things—to stand." Ephesians 6:11-13

One of the most lethal ways the enemy can come against us is as the Accuser. *"The methods of the Accuser"* are designed to weaken us by attacking our most sensitive and vulnerable areas. His schemes are devised to create doubt and fear, causing us to lose confidence in our salvation and hope. If our defenses can be breached, he will be able to send an invasion force to finish the job —unrighteous thoughts, leading to sinful deeds, then ultimately to a total falling-away from the Master.

It is easy to think that the greatest dangers we face are in the natural realm—situations that threaten our health or physical safety. In reality, however, *"we wrestle not with blood and flesh,"* but with *"the spiritual things of evil...."* There are forces and powers operating in realms that we cannot even begin to fathom, yet we interact with them on a daily basis. These principalities, authorities and rulers of darkness may be unseen to the naked eye, but they can certainly be discerned by the damage they inflict upon our overall spiritual health.

It is for this reason that we are exhorted to *"put on the whole armor of God."* The Accuser will come—and has come even now—to do war against those who live by the Spirit of Messiah. Even if we are hesitant to run into battle, the Accuser already has in mind to bring the fight to us. It is only when we are fully clad in the armor of God that we will be able to resist the evil when it is upon us, and not be crushed by the onslaught of darkness.

We are to *"take up the whole armor of God"*—not to fight, but to stand. We have been given other implements with which to do war, but the armor is there to keep us from taking a fall. With our vulnerable parts protected, the methods of the Accuser will not be able to penetrate our defenses and weaken our position. So let us put on God's armor, that we may resist in the day of evil… then, *"[after] having done all things—to stand."*

෨෬ ෧

Father, I bless Your Name and praise You for Your protection. Teach me to diligently put on the whole armor of God, so that my strength will not fail as I wrestle with the spiritual things of evil. Make me discerning, Lord, to be aware of the methods of the Accuser—to resist his schemes and treachery. But above all, ADONAI, I bless You, for You have clothed me in Your righteousness—and after everything is said and done, I will not fall… but stand.

Take Care to Do

"*Only, be strong and very courageous, to take care to do [everything] according to all the* תּוֹרָה, *Torah which* מֹשֶׁה, *Moshe My servant commanded you. Do not turn aside from it—right or left—so that you will act wisely in every* place *wherever you go. The book of this* תּוֹרָה, *Torah is not to depart out of your mouth, and you are to meditate on it by day and by night, so that you will take care to do [everything] according to all that is written in it. For then you will cause your way to prosper, and then you will act wisely.*" יְהוֹשֻׁעַ *Y'hoshua (Joshua) 1:7-8*

As Yis'rael was about to enter the Promised Land, it would have been natural to expect ADONAI to make her into a strong military power, able to overcome and defeat all her enemies through her great might. But instead of counseling Y'hoshua to look for strength in an army or courage in a fighting force, ADONAI told him to find these things by doing His Word.

The instructions ADONAI gave to Y'hoshua were crucial for his ability to lead Yis'rael into the Land. He was to always keep ADONAI's Word before him… "*do not turn aside from it—right or left….*" The Word of ADONAI was to constantly be on his lips… "*this Torah is not to depart out of your mouth….*" It was to be foremost in his mind at all times… "*meditate on it by day and by night.*" It would only be through such unceasing dedication to ADONAI's Word that Y'hoshua would succeed as the head of God's holy nation.

But there is a deeper purpose for this constant meditation—this unwavering focus—on the Word of ADONAI. Keeping God's Word always before us, in our mouths and on our minds, is only of value if we "*take care to do*" what it says. The Word has no power in our lives if we are not willing to carry out the instructions we are given.

When we act "*according to all that is written*" in God's Word, we will be able to successfully navigate through the course of life and succeed in everything we set out to do. Like Y'hoshua, we cannot rely on strategic battle plans or well-executed tactics to lead us to victory. When we are facing the opposing forces of life, our only hope for success is to "*take care to do [everything] according to all that is written.... then you will act wisely.*"

❧ ❧

Abba, Father, I want to be strong and courageous for You. Help me to keep Your Word before me—place it in my mouth and commit it to my mind, that I may do all that it tells me to do. Teach me to be mindful of Your Word—to "*take care to do*" it all the days of my life—that I may prosper in the way *You* have set out before me. I praise You, ADONAI, Giver of the Torah....

Material to Make

"Take away [the impure] dross from silver,
and a material for the [silver]smith [to use to
make a vessel] comes forth." מִשְׁלֵי Mish'lei
(Proverbs) 25:4

O, ADONAI! Why won't You bless me? Here I am
—I am willing to be used in Your service! I give myself
completely to You... so why do I still suffer? Why do
things still go wrong? Where is my peace and my joy?
Every day is full of trials, discouragement and failure.
Please, O God—I have forsaken everything to follow
only You! Lord? Did you speak to me? Yes, I hear You,
Father—what did You say? You say there are things I
have *not* forsaken to follow You? Which things, ADONAI?
Oh... *those* things. Well, I know you've mentioned them
to me before, but I've been serving you for so long
without getting rid of them—surely they're not *that*
detrimental to my walk with you. O Lord! Won't you
bless me? Here I am—use me... I am your servant!

Many of us cry out to the Lord to save us from our
dismal, unvictorious lives. We know we are in Messiah
—and we do have some sense of security in that—but
for some reason, we keep missing that abundant life
which has been promised to us. Why is this so? We pray,
we serve, we give an inordinate amount of time to God,
and still, we have no peace, no joy—no testimony of
Yeshua in our lives. Perhaps—just maybe—it is because
we have not been giving The Silversmith good material
with which to work.

"Take away [the impure] dross from silver..." We
are a fine material—rich and beautiful, a new creation
—but we have impurities in our lives that have not yet
been removed. Perhaps the reason we have not been
filled up is because we cannot yet be made into vessels
capable of holding what the Father is waiting to pour
into us. Is The Silversmith still waiting for *"material...
[to use to make a vessel]"* out of you?

A vessel made with *pure* material will be holy—set
apart for sacred use. A vessel made with *impure* material
will not be *holy*—it will just be *full of holes.* Today, ADONAI
wants to make you into a vessel—not one that will leak
out the bottom, but one that will hold its contents to
overflowing! What "dross" do you still have in your life?
What things need to be removed? You know what "those
things" are. Set them aside today—once and for all—and
The Silversmith will finally have the material to make a
truly wonderful vessel...

᠔᠂᠁

Abba, Father, I repent and lay myself bare before You
now. I am ready to be separated from my impurities, that
I may truly be a vessel worthy of Your service. Don't just
plug up my leaks, Father, but put me through the fire so
that I may be useful in Your kingdom. I bless You, My
God, for in Your hands, I am made into a glorious vessel
dedicated only to You. I praise You, ADONAI, the Purifying
Flame...

Though Not Having Seen

"...the proof of your faith (much more precious than of gold that is perishing, but through fire is proved) may be found in praise, and honor, and glory, in the revelation of Messiah Yeshua, whom ([though] not having seen [Him]) you love, [and] in whom ([though] not seeing [Him] now, nevertheless, [you] believe) you are glad with unspeakable joy, and [are] glorified, receiving the goal of your faith—[the] salvation of [your] souls."
כֵּיפָא א *Keifa Alef (1Peter) 1:7-9*

We have all had moments when we questioned or doubted our faith in Yeshua. Yet sometimes—especially in times of testing and tribulation—our faith in the invisible is the only thing to which we can cling. Of course, this is not always easy, and we need some reassurance— some undeniable proof—that our faith is not only well-placed, but grounded in Someone who is very, very real.

"[Though] not having seen [Him], you love [Him]." With only the written testimony of men from an age long past, and the unexplainable conviction deep down in your gut, somehow it's enough—you love Him. You've never seen Him with your own eyes; you've never heard the sound of His voice. You didn't witness His miracles;

you didn't sit at His feet. You didn't see Him suffer and die; you didn't behold Him after He was raised from the dead. And yet, for some reason, you love Him. That's proof.

"[Though] not seeing [Him] now, nevertheless, [you] believe." To this day, you commit your life to Him; you have devoted yourself to His service… but He does not appear to you. You lift up your voice in praise of His Name; you petition Him in prayer and seek His face… but His reply does not come with spoken words. You are filled with gladness—unspeakable joy—when you enter into His presence… but there is no tangible evidence of Him ever having been there with you. And yet, for some reason, you believe. That's proof.

The proof of our faith is that Messiah has been made known to us. We can take great comfort in knowing that what was once hidden has now been revealed—that we may love Him and believe with the assurance of genuine faith. Our unwavering faith in the invisible is all the proof we need! In this way, we receive *"the goal of [our] faith"* —and even though we have no evidence to appease our senses, we can fully place our trust in the Master for *"[the] salvation of [our] souls."*

જે ન્ક

Master, You are worthy of all praise, honor and glory, for though I cannot see You with my eyes, You have been revealed to me. I praise You, my God, for though I cannot hear You speak, I know Your voice— and I will follow and obey. I dedicate myself to Your service, O Mighty One of Yis'rael. I bless You, ADONAI, my King, for You cause me to trust—and even when You are apparently nowhere to be found, I am filled with joy in Your presence…

Prophetic Patience

"Woe to *those who draw out iniquity with cords of falsehood, and sin as with thick cart ropes. They say, 'Let [God] hurry, let Him hasten His work, that we may see, and let the counsel of the Holy One of* יִשְׂרָאֵל, *Yis'rael draw near and come, [so that] we [can] know.'*"
יְשַׁעְיָהוּ *Y'sha'yahu (Isaiah) 5:18-19*

When we think of patience, it is usually a patience that is colored with *tolerance*. It's not so much that we are *patient* with others, but that we are *tolerant* of their behavior—or lack of behavior—so we *wait*. But godly patience is very different, for it is birthed from *faith* and *obedience*. We don't wait on ADONAI because we are tolerating His delays, but because we trust His faithfulness. When He says, "Wait," we know that His timing is best —no matter how long-suffering it may seem at the time.

As we wait with a godly patience, the passage of time is easier to endure—we are able to prophetically see ADONAI's deliverance coming at an appropriate time in the future. This kind of patience empowers us to withstand temptation and avert distractions as we remain focused on ADONAI, His Word and His promises. With godly patience, we can be *certain* of God's plans even before they are completely revealed to us.

Yet all too often, this patience escapes our grasp. "Speed it up! Hurry it along! We want to see it! Come on, God, Creator of the universe, space and time... You're taking too long!"

We are toying with sin when we live without obedience and faith in God's timing for our futures. Having a prophetic understanding of what is to come does not give us an excuse to race forward in our own strength. Indeed, if we can't even wait when ADONAI says, "Wait," then how much more will our unheeding be when He says, "Go," or "Stop!"

When we learn godly patience, we learn the ways of ADONAI. This is the very nature of being *prophetic* —learning to take God at His every word. Through patience, we put our trust and faith into action as we submit to His *present will* for our lives. If we can only be patient, He will always—without fail—bring us exactly where He wants us to be.

ॐ ॐ

ADONAI, my only desire is to see You glorified! Father, I trust in Your timing—You have never fallen short or arrived too late. Thank You for showing me Your face, for letting me hear Your voice, and for giving me boldness to stand on Your promises. You are who You say You are, and You will do what You say You will do. I praise You, Lord, for Your plans will certainly all come to pass... and so I wait....

But I Remember

"To the ages, will אֲדֹנָי, Adonai reject [me]? Will He ever be pleased with me again? Has His kindness ceased forever? [His] word failed to all generations? Has God forgotten [to be] gracious? Has He withdrawn His mercies in anger? סֶלָה, Selah. And I say, 'My failure is [causing] the turning [away] of the right hand of עֶלְיוֹן, El'yon [the Most High].' [But] I remember the deeds of יָהּ, Yah, for I remember of old Your wonders. And I will meditate on all Your works, and speak forth thoughts [of] Your doings." תְּהִלִּם T'hillim (Psalms) 77:7-12

We have all gone through times of grief and despair with the Lord—some of us as recently as today. We hold our head in our hands, hoping beyond hope that somehow everything will just go away—praying that when we lift our heads again it will have all just been a bad dream. The guilt and shame becomes overwhelming, and we throw our hands up to Heaven, wondering where God could possibly be. "Where has He gone? Why isn't He here? Has Adonai rejected me forever?

"Will He ever be pleased with me again?" we inquire of ourselves. "Have I finally done it this time? Have I pushed Him away forever?" The apparent gravity of the situation finally begins to dawn on us. "Maybe there's more to what's going on here. What if God is not just unhappy with me—what if He's finally fed up? What if this isn't just some time of testing or character building, but He's really, actually gone? Is this right? Is this possible? *Has God forgotten [to be] gracious? Has He withdrawn His mercies in anger?*

"It's me. Oh no, it's me! I finally did it. I pushed Him away. I sinned one too many times; I failed to trust Him once more, and now He's had it. He's done with me! He's through! *My failure is [causing] the turning [away] of the right hand of El'yon.* It's all my fault, and now He's gone! I caused His hand of blessing to turn away from me because of my weakness and failure to live according to His righteous ways. How could I have done this? What have I *done*?

"*[But] I remember the deeds of Yah.*"

It's one thing to live in awesome fear of El'yon, but it's quite another to beat ourselves up for sins that He is surely willing and able to forgive. To avoid being stricken with grief and plummeting into the pit of despair, we must remember the deeds of Yah—to meditate on them and speak forth the mighty things He has done. Then, though we may sometimes feel like we're getting the back of the hand, we will be able to recall His mighty deeds… and it won't be long before we realize that we were never far from His loving embrace.

છ જ્જ

El'yon, Most High, I remember Your deeds, I recall Your wonders of old. Cause me to meditate on all Your works and speak forth thoughts of Your doings, that I may forever remember Your faithfulness. Thank You, ADONAI, for not turning Your hand from me, and for waiting patiently until I turn toward You. Yah, I bless Your Holy Name, for You show grace and mercy forever…

Like Apples of Gold

"[Like] apples of gold in settings of silver is a word spoken in its [appropriate] circumstances. [Like] a ring of gold, and an ornament of pure gold, is the wise reprover to a hearing ear." מִשְׁלֵי Mish'lei (Proverbs) 25:11-12

As disciples of Messiah, we have the serious responsibility to give reproof and correction to a brother who has fallen. At first glance, we might think that this proverb is promoting a soft, delicate approach to giving such reproof—that we are to "love" the person back to right relationship with God. But while it is absolutely true that correction must always be given with love, that is *not* the point we are being taught in this instance. Though all correction is to be delivered with love, the words we speak must be appropriate to the situation.

This is what is means to be a *"wise reprover."* One is wise when he gives a reproof that fits the need for correction. In some cases, this may very well mean being soft-spoken and gentle. However, there are other times—perhaps more often than we care to admit—that correction needs to be brought with much strength and authority. A brother who has simply wandered off the path may only need a slight nudge to get him back on track—but a brother who is helplessly lost in rebellion may need great force to break his stubborn pride and rip the veil of blindness and denial from his eyes.

The goal in bringing correction is to find a *"hearing ear"*—one that is receptive and will hear the reproof without taking offense. While a harsh voice can sometimes cause a hearing ear to turn *deaf*, there are other times that a brother needs to be jolted back to reality in order to see the error of his ways. Wisdom—together with love—dictates the right words to say, when to say them, and how they are to be said.

A *"word spoken in its [appropriate] circumstances"* is like fine gold and silver—it is a priceless treasure. As such, it is also delicate enough to be crushed under the weight of our own understanding if we offer reproof in our own wisdom. The truly wise man will yield himself to God, speaking the appropriate word of reproof according to the Spirit. Indeed, this is our only hope of bringing restoration—even when it is not the time, the place, or the way *we* would choose....

ADONAI, teach me to be a wise reprover who speaks in appropriate circumstances according to Your ways. Show me, Lord, how to hear Your voice at all times, and to only speak the words You want me to say. I praise You, Abba, for through Your wisdom and love, men are corrected and restored to You. Thank You, Father, for helping me to yield and submit to Your wisdom, and to do only as You will....

Bear Fruit

*"Therefore, [if you are truly confessing your sins,] bear fruits worthy of reformation (repentance). Do not think [you are saved by your lineage] and say to yourselves, "We have a father—*אַבְרָהָם*, Av'raham!" For I say to you, that God is able to raise children to* אַבְרָהָם*, Av'raham out of these stones. And now also, the axe is laid to the root of the trees. Therefore, every tree not bearing good fruit will be cut off and cast into fire."* מַתִּתְיָהוּ *Matit'yahu (Matthew) 3:8-10*

When the Pharisees and Sadducees approached Yochanan to be immersed, he had hard words for them —and we would do well to take them to heart ourselves. Not unlike many Jews and Christians of today, the Pharisees and Sadducees considered themselves "saved" by virtue of lineage—that is, by their ethnic or religious membership. Thus, the Pharisees and Sadducees lived their lives as those who considered themselves "in" by default. Yet ultimately, some sought out Yochanan in the hopes of *"flee[ing] the coming wrath."* (vs. 7)

Yochanan warned the Pharisees and Sadducees that they should not be too confident of their salvation by virtue of their father, Av'raham, because there is no eternal security in physical lineage. Indeed, as Yochanan says, *"God is able to raise children to Av'raham out of… stones!"* Yet a Gentile believer certainly shouldn't think he has a higher level of security than the natural descendants of Av'raham, for *"every tree not bearing good fruit will be cut off and cast into fire."*

Here is the bottom line: if one is truly repentant, having confessed all his sins, then he must *"bear fruits worthy of reformation."* At one time or another, every believer has silently judged another by his fruit—or lack thereof—thinking, "So and so is not really saved." However, we would do well to turn such a critical eye upon ourselves, realizing that others may well have had sufficient evidence to judge us in the same manner.

We are the ones who will benefit from this self-exam, for ADONAI already knows our hearts—and He sees the fruit that we will or will not bear in the future. So ask yourself the question, "Have I really turned from my sins to God?"—and answer yourself by taking a hard look at the fruit in your life. Are you bearing good fruit? Praise ADONAI! But if you are bearing bad fruit, or none at all, now you can determine to walk differently from this moment on. Just remember that your ethnic or religious membership cannot save you—we must all look to Yeshua, for He alone is our salvation.

ॐ ॐ

ADONAI, help me to check my heart, my mind, and my actions; teach me Your ways, that my life will bear evidence of truly turning to You. Thank You, Abba, for choosing me and making me Your own. Show me how to live according to Your Word—how to abide in Your love and bear good fruit. I praise You, O God, for You are my salvation. I am Your child, raised out of the stones—help me to continue in Your righteousness....

Shut Up

*"You have deceived me, O ADONAI, and
I am deceived; You have overcome me and
prevailed. I have been laughed at all the day;
everyone is mocking at me, because from the
moment I [begin to] speak, I cry out, 'Violence!'
and 'Destruction!' I proclaim. So the word of
ADONAI has brought to me reproach and
ridicule all the day. But [if] I say, 'I will not
mention Him, nor will I speak anymore in His
Name,' [His word] will be in my heart as a
burning fire, shut up in my bones. I am weary
of holding [it in, indeed] I am not able."*
יִרְמְיָהוּ *Yir'm'yahu (Jeremiah) 20:7-9*

Perhaps our greatest underlying fear is that this faith
we have in Yeshua is only a pipedream, a mirage, a myth.
Of course, we never say this out loud—and maybe we
don't even give it much conscious thought—but why
else do we hold back from sharing Yeshua everywhere
we go? All too often, we lack a hardcore conviction that
He is Messiah, and so the thought of proclaiming Him
to everyone we meet strikes us with panic and dread.
We seal our lips and go on our way, and we are none
the worse for it…. Or are we?

If there was ever a man in Yis'rael who had a reason
to keep his mouth shut, it was Yir'm'yahu. Every time
he opened his mouth to speak, it was far more than the
blasé, "Have you accepted the Messiah Yeshua as your
personal Lord and Savior?" No, his cry was, *"Violence!"*

and *"Destruction!"* to the people of Yis'rael. As a result, did they repent and turn to God? Hardly. Instead, they laughed at the prophet and mocked him. For this, Yir'm'yahu felt he had been swindled by the Lord into his wretched existence. He said, *"the word of ADONAI has brought to me reproach and ridicule all the day."*

Having experienced such insult and injury, who would have blamed Yir'm'yahu if he kept quiet, watching knowingly as his brothers walked closer to punishment and wrath each day? But instead, he resigned himself to his fate—that the word of ADONAI would burn unceasingly in his heart despite any attempts to still his tongue. Yir'm'yahu was *"overcome"* by the power of the word of God—he had *no choice* but to speak in ADONAI's name.

Is the truth of the Messiah Yeshua a *"burning fire"* in *your* heart today? Instead of shying away from proclaiming His Name by saying, *"I am not able,"* we should be so unbelievably compelled to proclaim the Good News that we cry out, *"'I am not able' to stop!"* Let us no longer be *"weary"* of confronting people with the truth and love of Messiah—instead, may it be so *"shut up in [our] bones"* that we become *"weary of holding [it in]!"*

ॐ ॐ

ADONAI, my God—overcome me. Prevail over my flesh, and put Your word in my mouth. Unseal my lips, O Holy One of Yis'rael, and ignite a burning fire in my heart that cannot be contained. Make me *unable*, Lord —*unable* to be fearful of speaking Your Name... and *unable* to hold it in. I praise You, ADONAI, for it is in You that all may find life. Give me no choice, Father, but to tell everyone, everywhere, the truth of Your great Name...

*"You have set our iniquities before you,
our hidden things in the light of your face."*
תְּהִלִּם *T'hillim (Psalms) 90:8*

Do you remember the condition of your life before
you knew Yeshua? Do you recall the things you used to
do, the way you used to think, the things you used to say?
Do you remember when Yeshua got a hold of you, how
those areas of your life just fell away—thick, hardened
layers of caked-on filth crumbled from your new creation
self—and you were released into a life of freedom for
the Messiah?

And do you also remember that first moment when
you realized that there was still some gunk stuck in those
hard-to-reach places? Do you recall how the euphoria
began to dissipate as you discovered that underneath all
that crust, there was still a coating of flesh clinging to
you? Do you remember how you tried for a while to
scrape and scrub it off, but to no avail—it seemed that,
after all, there were some sins that you just couldn't
shake?

It is at this moment of realization that we all begin
to panic. Fearful of being found out, we do our best to
conceal our sins and put on a pious face for our friends
and family. Yet as we hide our sins away, keeping others
from seeing them (or so we think), *we* also forget that
they are there. When they eventually get around to
rearing their ugly little heads once again, we deny that

they belong to us—we are blind and truly unable to discern.

But there is One who discerns all, and He is blind to nothing. There is no place secret enough to keep our sins hidden from ADONAI. Indeed, He sets our iniquities before Him, and *"our hidden things in the light of [His] face."* He already knows the sins to which we have re-enslaved ourselves, even when we can't admit to our own bondage.

We can attempt to live in the shadows, but it will benefit no one. Only when we expose ourselves to the intense light of ADONAI's presence—enduring the temporary pain as our flesh is burned away—will we finally be healed and set free. No longer in darkness, we are now able to live and grow in a manner worthy of one who carries the name, "Yeshua's."

So where do you want to live in relation to the Light? Are you going to keep darting between the shadows, hoping to go unnoticed—or will you step into the purifying presence of the One who offers complete salvation?

ঔ ৵

ADONAI, I am unable to remain in the darkness any longer! You know my iniquities, the sins I have tried to keep hidden. Lord, I want to live in Your righteousness; help me to stop acting like the person I was before, and start living as the person You have remade me to be! ADONAI, teach me to trust that being exposed before You is far better than being hidden from Your presence. Let Your Light shine brightly on me, O God, because it's time for me to finally stop living in the shadows…

Come Up Here

"*Do not honor yourself before a king, and stand not in the place of the great. For [it is] better for you to be told, 'Come up here,' than to be humiliated before a nobleman, whom your eyes have seen.*" מִשְׁלֵי *Mish'lei (Proverbs) 25:6-7*

There is a private room. You are dying to go in because you know that what goes on behind that closed door is where you belong. This is where the leaders, men of renown, are making decisions, discussing things of great importance and monumental proportions. You want desperately to be in that meeting—you know that you have so much to offer, so much help to give. In your heart, you are certain that you, too, have a *"place [among] the great."* The only problem is that no one knows it but you.

We human beings often picture ourselves as greater than others see us. This comes from a thing called Pride. Motivations aside, we have a tendency to want to be "in the know"—to be part of the group that people respect and look up to as important. In truth, some people most certainly deserve to be part of that group, and they have the potential to make a profound impact in their spheres of influence. But Wisdom has words for one who would take his place presumptuously.

"Do not honor yourself before a king..." The fastest way to disqualify oneself from a place among the great is self-promotion. Sure, you may be able to sneak your

way into the room, perhaps even find yourself sitting at the table. But as soon as you open your mouth to espouse your great wisdom, everyone will ask, "Who *is* this?" and you will be ushered out, *"humiliated before a nobleman."*

It is not what we think of ourselves that will earn us a place before the king—it is our willingness to serve in anonymity. The one who serves with a pure heart that is void of selfish ambition, he will certainly be noticed as the noblemen walk to and from the private room. Then, everyone will ask, "Who is *this*?" and you will be invited in, *"for [it is] better for you to be told, 'Come up here,'"* then to be exposed as a poseur. Humble service is a bright light that shines on greatness, and the King will raise up the one who desires only to lift others first.

ॐ ॐ

Father, I ask for You to teach me to be humble—to truly desire service to You above recognition and prestige. Thank You, Abba, for putting a servant's heart within me—for showing me what it means to put others' needs above my own—because this is how the Truly Great One lived. I praise You ADONAI, for giving Your servant Yeshua—break me and mold me, that I may be more like Your Son....

Rebuke the Wind

"And there came a severe windstorm, and the waves were beating on the boat, so that it was already being filled. But [Yeshua] himself was in the stern on a pillow, sleeping, and [the disciples] woke Him up and said to him, 'Teacher, do you not care that we [are about to] die?' And having awakened, He rebuked the wind and said to the sea, 'Quiet! Be still!' and the wind died down, and there was a great calm."
Mark 4:37-39

I like to imagine Yeshua sound asleep, resting peacefully on His comfortable cushion when He is abruptly—and rudely—jarred awake by His untrusting disciples. I imagine Him looking up sleepily at the disciples, annoyed that He is now awake. The sound of the waves and the wind begin to come into focus, and the Master grumbles something to Himself about "What is *with* these guys?" and "Can't get a good night's sleep to save your life...." Sitting up on one arm, He groggily says, *"Quiet! Be still!"* and the wind subsides to a dead calm. The disciples don't even realize that, in part, He was talking to them. After another brief word of chastisement, Yeshua lays back down and begins to drift off into the peace of sleep once again. The disciples gape at their slumbering Savior and each other, utterly dumbfounded.

Even half-asleep, the Master displayed such power and faith that we still marvel at Him today. Yet we are His disciples! Shouldn't we have such confidence and trust in Him that a little wind and water wouldn't even wake us from a light sleep? But many of us continue to struggle just like the Twelve. We don't seem to understand that what we see with our eyes and hear with our ears doesn't really matter. We have power and authority that comes from the Master, and we are able and entitled to exercise them.

The key is in our Teacher's words, *"Quiet! Be still!"* We will never be able to handle the waves of life if we panic every time something unexpected or bad happens. Indeed, what lesson was Yeshua teaching His disciples? To take authority over and rebuke those things that frighten us? Or, to *learn* that we don't have to be afraid of things that can't really hurt us? Maybe a little of both. It seems the Master's preference that night would have been for the disciples to ignore the ruckus and go back to sleep.

Ultimately, the Father is like every good parent—He wants us to come to Him each and every time we need Him. But also like a good parent, He wants us to grow up and mature—to deal with life as an adult. He loves to help us and care for us, but just think how proud He will be when we rebuke the wind ourselves....

҈ ҉

ADONAI, I bless You and praise You, for You have given me the ability to be quiet in the midst of chaos— to be still in the middle of turmoil. Teach me Your ways, that I may learn to rest where others panic, and to trust in You, fearing nothing. Thank You, Father, for growing me to maturity and showing me the ways of peace....

I Live No More

"With Messiah I have been crucified, and I live no more, but Messiah lives in me. And [the life] which I now live in the flesh, I live in the faith of the Son of God, who loved me and gave Himself for me." Galatians 2:20

As people of faith, we like to think of ourselves as worshippers or followers, but we usually try to avoid describing ourselves with the term "religious." Religiosity carries with it a negative connotation—we don't want to be motivated by some staunch, "dead" religion, but by a faithful, spiritual relationship. Yet even so, we are still inclined to compartmentalize our faith, making it merely one of life's components among many. In other words, we allow just enough room on the palette of our life to comfortably fit our *religion*.

But we have it completely backwards! Our faith in Messiah was never meant to be *incorporated* into our preexisting lives, for *"with Messiah [we] have been crucified, and [we] live no more...."* We are dead, and with that death should go all our ideas, priorities, and preferences. Our new life in Messiah was never intended to *improve* our old one, but to *kill* it. Then, when we were raised with Him, *He* would live in *us*—and *we* would live no more.

The life that we now live is not our own. It has been bought and paid for, now belonging to someone else. What was crucified has been made alive again—but not so that we may simply resume our lives with a special place in our hearts for God. *"The faith of the Son of God"* was never supposed to become the "religious" part of our lives that we can choose to integrate or exclude as we deem fit. The life that we *"now live in the flesh"* has been recreated for a new purpose—no longer to serve ourselves, but to serve the King.

We live in newness of life today because the Son of God—the Messiah Yeshua—*"loved [us] and gave Himself for [us]."* He was crucified, not for His sake, but for ours! He loved us so much that He took our old selves with Him in death, that we might be raised with Him to live forever. Yeshua demonstrated His love by giving His life for us. Perhaps it is time for us to start giving back a little of ourselves.

ॐ ॐ

Master, I could never repay what You have already done for me, so the least I can do is give You everything I have. Thank You for giving Yourself for me so that I will live no more—and I live again to serve only You. I praise You, ADONAI, for Your salvation. Please teach me to set myself aside, so that Messiah may live in me. Thank You for loving me, Father, and for sending Your Son... in whom I now live...

Give Me a Thought

"Of whom have you been afraid and feared,
that you [have] lied and not remembered Me?
You do not give [Me] a thought! Have I been
silent for so long that you no [longer] fear Me?"
יְשַׁעְיָהוּ *Y'sha'yahu (Isaiah) 57:11*

Even the greatest of sinners waits until it's dark and he is in private before fully indulging himself. His "morality" is what he shows in the light, in the daytime when he is among others. But when the light of day fades, he retreats to his secret place—and behind closed doors, he performs acts against ADONAI.

This inclination of humankind toward evil is founded on the belief that there is only one reality—the one we can experience with our tactile senses. Who would consider themselves unseeable if they believed in a God who could see all things? And yet, the spiritual world is just as real as the physical—and it is in the spirit that we are seen doing our most dastardly deeds.

So why do any of us think that we can sin in private and get away with it? Just because our families and friends don't know about it—and may never find out—that doesn't mean God hasn't seen. Indeed, it is in the secret place that God meets us—and it is our choice whether to make the secret place holy or profane.

We have no fear of God because we *forget* He is there. When we fail to seek Him, He withdraws and watches us sin—with growing contempt—keeping silent. And we don't even give Him a thought… "Is this holy? Is this a sin? What would He say if He were here?" We may think we can simply hide from His presence, but the truth is that He is ever-present… and He never misses a thing.

ॐ ॐ

ADONAI, I am ashamed of the sins of my hands—especially those that I have committed behind closed doors. Forgive me, Father… I have forgotten You when I should have been fearing You. Lord, thank You for washing me clean of my sins and welcoming me back into Your arms. Teach me to never forget that You are always here—not to sit in judgment, but to guide me into truth, to bless me, and to keep me holy before a holy God. Thank You, Father—I want to be holy as You are holy….

Every Word of God's

"*Every word of God's is purified, a shield He is to those trusting in Him. Add not to His words, lest He rebuke you, and you be found a liar.*" מִשְׁלֵי *Mish'lei (Proverbs) 30:5-6*

How can we survive without the purity of God's word? In what can we place our trust? Can we truly depend on our own abilities? Can we rely on our own spiritual insights? How can we have confidence in our own experiences and ways of thinking—ideas which are flawed at best? There is only one way: by lining everything up with the pure Word of God.

The pure Word of God is a refuge which shields us from the deceptions of our own mind and flesh. It is the perfect standard to determine if the things we *believe* we perceive are the truth or a lie. If our experience varies even the slightest degree from the Word of God, we are wrong... we are deceived. The Word of God is unchanging and perfectly consistent—even when our own lives are full of inconsistencies.

Yet it is a great temptation to "*add... to His words,*" thereby weakening our own protection. We do this when we piece together unrelated or remotely similar portions of Scripture in order to glean "new" spiritual understanding. Or, we take passages out of context and apply them to our circumstances in an attempt to bring about a sense of peace or comfort in our lives. But the Word of God is not a "magic 8-ball" that we can shake until we get the answers we want—we cannot contrive or manipulate the Word until our spirits testify to what it says. The Word, taken without addition, is more than enough for answering every question, providing perfect protection, and giving sound direction.

When we accept anything other than every pure Word of God, we "*add… to His words,*" and "*He [will] rebuke you, and you be found a liar.*" Trusting in His pure Word is far more than just holding onto a particular set of verses that happen to be speaking to our lives right now. Indeed, *every* Word of God's is pure! We can take great solace in knowing that even when we don't understand, if we obey and submit our lives to His Word, we will *always* be led into the truth—the whole truth, and nothing but the truth…

ॐ ॐ

ADONAI, I know that I am susceptible to every kind of spirit and teaching when I am not protected by Your Word. I never want to require Your rebuke, nor to be found a liar. Abba, teach me to truly test everything with the whole, complete, pure Word of God—and help me to resist any thought or spirit that strays even a little from Your Scriptures. Show me, Lord, how to immediately recognize the Spirit of God speaking to me. Plant Your Word so deep inside me that I will be able to instantly confirm what the Spirit is saying with Your pure, holy, and perfect Word.…

Et'patach אֶפָּתַח
(Be Opened)

"And they brought to [Yeshua] a deaf man [who had] difficulty speaking, and they called on Yeshua that He may lay His hand on the man. And taking the man by himself away from the crowd, [Yeshua] put His fingers into the man's ears, spat, and touched his tongue. And looking to the Heavens, [Yeshua] groaned and said to him, אֶפָּתַח, Et'patach!' that is, 'Be opened!' and immediately the man's ears opened, and the binding of his tongue was loosed, and he [began] speaking correctly."
Mark 7:32-35

Ok… that's just a *tad* weird… and gross…. I sort of get the part about the fingers in the ears, and touching the tongue, but what's with the *spit*? Even so, you would think the Master would be a *little* more concerned with *hygiene*… who *knows* what kind of germs might be hiding in there…. Did He really have to be so *invasive*? Why not just a simple *"Et'patach!"* and then send the man on his way?

Perhaps the most wonderful events recorded in the Word are those things that completely and utterly baffle our sense of what is reasonable, acceptable and normal. Either Yeshua performed this particular healing exactly the way it needed to be done, or He didn't. Who is to say? What we can be sure of is this: there is not a thing wrong with sticking your finger in a deaf man's ears when praying for his healing!

This, of course, is not a license for strange and bizarre behavior going unchecked—running rampant through the Body of Messiah. But Yeshua was not scampering around like a mad man spitting on people and sticking His fingers in their ears. The Master was performing a miracle! Is not a *miracle*, in the strictest sense, *strange and bizarre*? A bona fide miracle is beyond science, medicine, reason and understanding. It confounds the wisest of people.

When we close our hearts and minds to anything outside our comfort zone—anything beyond our understanding of what is right and proper—we shut ourselves off from healing, miracles, and other spiritual work from ADONAI. We cannot be afraid to allow the Lord to interact with us—not only in our minds, but in our spirits … in our whole beings. The Master is groaning for His people today, saying, *"Et'patach!"* ("Be opened!") He wants to move among us and through us, that He may be glorified and His salvation brought to the ends of the earth.

ॐ ॐ

Father, I trust You, though I do not always understand Your ways. Teach me to yield myself to You, and to be willing to step outside—*way* outside—my comfort zone. I praise You, ADONAI, for giving me the ability to lay hands on the sick, to perform miracles in Your Name… to live a spiritual life. Thank You, O God, for Your great and wonderful ways. You are worthy of all my praise….

For Doing Anything Good

"All things, indeed, are pure to [those who are] pure, but to those defiled [with sins] and unbelieving, nothing is pure—of them, even the mind and the conscience are defiled. They profess to know God, but in their actions, they deny Him. [They are] abominable and disobedient, and unfit for doing anything good."
Titus 1:15-16

Most of the time, we do a nice job of putting on a good face. Whether we are in some kind of need, some kind of crisis, or some kind of sin, we know very well how to avoid letting on. Often accompanying that exterior façade are words of faith and hopefulness. From talking to us, no one would know what we're really thinking—we make professions of faith with our mouths, but behind everyone's back, we are living a secret life… a life of fear and doubt.

How we manage to deceive others and ourselves with this performance is mind-boggling, yet we seem to have a knack for it. With our lips we speak of God's greatness, His sovereignty and provision, His faithfulness and salvation. But in our secret life, we doubt God and question His abilities. We become fist-shakers and curse-makers, unable to trust God for anything—all the while professing to know Him, and believing with all our heart that we do.

We are known by how we know God—yet this knowing is not determined by our words, but by our actions. We can give praise to ADONAI with every breath, all the while denying Him with the way we live. When we act according to our unbelief or disobedience, we defile ourselves and make ourselves abominable in God's sight. When we deny the power and character of our God, we ourselves become *"unfit for doing anything good."* The word of our testimony becomes invalid.

And yet, we have great hope, because *"all things, indeed,* are *pure to [those] who are pure..."* When we believe the word of our testimony and act upon it through obedience, we will know the purity that comes from truly knowing God. Our actions are to be a reflection of the profession we make with our mouths, that we may be pure and useful workers for the Kingdom. Though the mind and conscience may be defiled through disbelief, they can be made pure again by acting upon our faith. Let us boldly profess to know God... and then in our actions, affirm Him.

☙ ❧

In all things, ADONAI, may I know only purity and faith. Keep from me unbelief and disobedience, and cause me to trust and follow Your ways. I praise You ADONAI, for You have made me fit for service. Even in my mind and my conscience, Father, let me know You so that I may affirm Your greatness. I bless Your Name, for You are nothing but pure—lead me, Lord, into Your presence....

War and Peace

*"The prophets who have been before me
and before you, from of old, even they prophesied—concerning many lands, and concerning
great kingdoms—of war, and of calamity, and
of plague. [But] the prophet who prophesies of
peace—[only] when the word of the prophet
comes [true] is [it] known [of] the prophet that
ADONAI has truly sent him."* יִרְמְיָהוּ *Yir'm'yahu
(Jeremiah) 28:8-9*

Yir'm'yahu had quite the job in Yis'rael. Not only
did he have the pleasure of predicting Yis'rael's foreboding
doom, but he also got to pick apart his fellow prophets
who were foretelling otherwise. After hurling accusations
against the prophets *"who wag their [own] tongues"* (23:31),
Yir'm'yahu eventually singled out 'Chanan'yah, who
prophesied the soon return of Y'hudah from her exile in
Babylon. Two months later, the false prophet 'Chanan'yah
was dead.

Yir'm'yahu characterized the role of the prophet as
one who prophesied *"war... calamity... and plague."*
But who needs *that?* Who wants to hear that their dismal
situation is just going to get worse? Who wants to hear a
word from God without hope? Yet from Yir'm'yahu's
perspective, such a message is not hopeless—it gives
direction. The job of the prophet is not to make us feel
all warm and fuzzy inside while we continue in our sinful
ways—his job is to help us see where we're headed if we
don't shape up.

And yet, we want nothing to do with this "doom and gloom." The people of Yis'rael *begged* the prophets for a "good" word from ADONAI. To this, Yir'm'yahu responds, *"The prophet who prophesies of peace—[only] when the word of the prophet comes [true] is [it] known [of] the prophet that ADONAI has truly sent him."* According to Yir'm'yahu, there is a greater burden of proof on the prophet who prophesies *"peace,"* than one who prophesies *"war."*

When we speak words of encouragement to one another, let us take heed that we are indeed speaking the word of ADONAI, and not *"speak[ing] visions from [our] own [hearts and] minds"* (23:16). Instead of babbling on with our own empty words of hope and affirmation, may we hold our tongues until ADONAI releases them with words of righteousness and truth. Let us not seek to condemn one another, but to lift one another up by speaking the true word of ADONAI —giving direction and hope through *His* message, be it *"calamity"* or *"peace."*

☙ ❧

ADONAI, Your word alone is truth—my thoughts are nothing. When I speak, Lord, may I not fool myself into believing that my words are from You. Instead, Father, teach my tongue to hold still until You open my mouth to speak Your truth. I praise You, ADONAI, for even a prophet is not above Your correction and rebuke. Speak, ADONAI, that I may hear Your word and proclaim it—that my mouth will pronounce only direction and hope, holiness and comfort... according to *Your* perfect peace...

You Can Go Your Own Way

"[The] discipline of ADONAI, my son, do not despise, And be not irritated with His reproof, For whom ADONAI loves He reproves, Even as a father [reproves] the son He is pleased with." מִשְׁלֵי *Mish'lei (Proverbs) 3:11-12*

While not an extremely popular notion in our culture, the idea of self-discipline or self-control at least carries with it positive connotations. On the other hand, the idea of discipline in the form of reproof or correction by another entity—control, if you will—is almost always viewed as negative. In many minds, discipline is oppressive, domineering, and cruel. Any form of punishment is seen as a means of bringing a person under submission, making him weak and compliant.

One of mankind's greatest errors is believing that we are capable of disciplining ourselves. This way of thinking puts us in the place of God. When we believe that we have the capacity of our own volition to not only choose between right and wrong, but to also keep ourselves from errant behavior, we set ourselves up as gods. We do, indeed, resent it when others correct us.

But a truly disciplined life can only come from ADONAI. Sometimes His discipline may be administered through difficult times, when the natural mind would translate "trials" into punishment. Yet no matter how painful such correction may be, it is always for our benefit. ADONAI is like a father who is pleased with his son. He is delighted to correct us—to not spare the rod —for He knows that if we will not despise it, we will find wisdom, peace, and long life.

By receiving ADONAI's discipline, we know that He loves us, for a father does not discipline those who are not his own. Yielding and submitting to ADONAI is not enslavement to oppression, but surrender to abundant life. So when reproof comes, do not despise it and do not be irritated… for surely the Father is pleased with you.

೧೨ ೨

Abba, teach me to not despise Your discipline or be irritated with Your reproof. Your correction protects me and shows me the path to life. Thank You, Abba, for loving me and being pleased with me—and for not letting me go my own way. I bless You, ADONAI, Creator, Master, Father…

Growing Up in Prayer

"And I say to you, Ask, and it will be given to you; seek, and you will find; knock, and it will be opened to you; for everyone who asks will receive; and he who seeks will find; and to him who knocks it will be opened." Luke 11:9-10

Perseverance in prayer… the Master teaches us that nothing is outside our reach. Indeed, we have all experienced the miraculous results of prayer, though it may be only a distant memory. Still, Yeshua clearly teaches that persistent prayer yields consistent results. So why, even when we pray, does it seem like God is not moving on our behalf? Where is the fulfillment of this promise in our lives?

Anyone who has children knows that young people are capable of being extremely *persistent*, in a word. In their perseverance, they may eventually receive what they ask for… but not necessarily because it is *given* to them—sometimes, their parents just *give in*. Is Yeshua teaching us that if we *disturb* the Father long enough, He will eventually succumb to our whining and give us what we want—just to get us to be quiet?

It is more likely that the correct picture of perseverance in prayer is painted with *maturity*—the reason we do not receive is because we're asking from a limited perspective. Like children standing in a crowd, we are not tall enough to see over peoples' heads, but we are forced to stare at the back of their knees. Given this point of view, we can only see what is directly in front of us—and to our young minds, that is all that exists. But as we grow up, our perspective changes. We are able to see the same things more clearly—literally from a different height.

God deals with us "where we're at," but he also expects and helps us to mature. As we grow, we eventually stop asking for what *we* want and start asking for what *He* wants—and it is then that we *receive*. As our perspective changes, we start seeing things as they truly are, instead of the way we would like them to be—and it is then that we *find* what we are seeking. And when we become mature, we stop *pounding* on all the wrong doors and start *knocking* on the right one—and it is then that the door is finally *opened*.

ॐ ॐ

Yeshua, I receive Your promises to me. Help me to grow, and teach me to walk in humble maturity. Let me see things through Your eyes, and show me how to put childish things behind me. I desire to see You move sovereignly in my life each day. Enable me to be persistent in my prayer life, teach me to persevere, and help me to trust that You see everything—even when I can't see a thing...

*"In those days there was no king in יִשְׂרָאֵל,
Yis'rael; each did that which was right in his
own eyes."* שֹׁפְטִים *Shof'tiym (Judges) 21:25*

This final comment of *Shof'tiym* sums up the entire
saga of the judges. From one leader to the next, God
would hear the cries of the people of Yis'rael, raise up a
deliverer, and Yis'rael would live in peace and prosperity
for a time. But soon enough, the people—devoid of any
kingly authority—would begin to go their own way, fall
to their foes, and cry out once again to God for their
salvation.

"...each did that which was right in his own eyes."
God has given us the ability to think for ourselves.
Consequently, our natural tendency is to elevate our
own thoughts to a god-like plane, fooling ourselves into
putting undue faith in our own capabilities. As we then
step outside the lines of accountability and authority,
we become rogue, reckless, and able to do much
harm—to others as much as ourselves.

The presence of authority seems to have no lasting
effect when it is merely *imposed* upon us—we will still
follow our own desires as soon as we are able to subvert
it. So it is, too, with accountability—in its absence, our
flesh will quickly run away with us. It is only when we

deliberately choose to be self-submitting that the presence of authority and accountability can affect our thoughts and actions in any meaningful way.

This is why the Master intended for His disciples to live together in *community*. The accountability, support, and protection of our fellow believers brings balance to our otherwise egocentric existence. Doing whatever one thinks is right is impossible in this context, for we all adhere to the same set of instructions—the Scriptures —empowered by the same Spirit through the same Messiah, Yeshua. Our individual tendencies to fall to one side or the other are hampered, because we are standing shoulder-to-shoulder with one another.

As we collectively turn from our own ways through relationships of *accountability*, we will be able to submit to the *authority* of the One who rules. When we submit to the authority of the King, we receive His royal protection, provision and deliverance. We no longer simply do whatever we think is right—because in *this* day, there *is* a king in Yis'rael.

☙ ❧

King Messiah, I submit my will to You and receive Your salvation. Teach me to rely on others through relationships of accountability, that we may together walk in Your ways and avoid our destruction. Show me how to guard against the hurtful desires of my flesh, and increase my desire to walk in holiness before You. Thank You, Father, for Your protection and provision. I praise You and worship You, my King….

Things I Did Not Steal

"Those [who] hate me without cause have been more than the hairs of my head. Mighty have been my destroyers, my lying enemies. Things I did not steal, I return." תְּהִלִּם *T'hillim (Psalms) 69:4*

At one time or another, we have all felt unjustly accused about something we didn't do. Sometimes, a little bit of paranoia can go a long way in helping us theorize conspiracies against us. In David's case, however, he wasn't just imagining things. In a very real way, people were out to get him.

If there is one thing in life that the righteous man can count on, it's that he will have enemies bent on his destruction. Not only that, there will be a *lot* of them—*"more than the hairs of my head."* The righteous one may *think* he is hated *"without cause,"* but this is far from reality. He has indeed caused the hatred against himself—by his righteous ways, his integrity, and his relentless dedication to the truth.

Because of this, the righteous man tends to attract a special breed of enemy—the liars. On the lips of a liar, even our most righteous deeds can be made to resemble the most loathsome acts. A reputation can be utterly decimated with the aid of a few well-placed deceptions or half-truths—leaving us holding the bag for crimes we didn't commit. Before we know it, we are making compensation for damage we did not inflict, repenting for transgressions we did not make, and returning *"things [we] did not steal…"*

When we walk in the ways of righteousness, our enemies will abound, and we may be called upon to give back things we have never taken. But this is the very essence of a Messianic life—a life that willingly accepts punishment for the sins of others. As we return things we did not steal, let us remember that we are following the One who gave back everything that rightfully belonged to Him.

Father, my enemies have multiplied before me. Strengthen me, O God, to endure the pain of returning things I did not steal, giving back though I have taken nothing. I praise You, ADONAI, for sending Your Son, who has selflessly returned life where death was deserved. Teach me the ways of righteousness, Holy One—that I, too, may have the honor of living according to Your ways, and being hated without cause…

"Many are *the plans in a man's heart,*
but the purposes of ADONAI *will stand."*
מִשְׁלֵי *Mish'lei (Proverbs) 19:21*

People make many plans in their heart for one
simple reason—control. We want a sense of control
over our lives and destinies.

For some of us, this means trying to plan ahead for
every possible contingency—scheming for the myriad
of potential events that could be put into motion, all
hanging delicately on our next action. This person's
motto may be, "Plan for everything, and you'll be ready
for anything." But who has the mind of ADONAI, that
every unexpected variable may be accounted for? Making
well-thought-out plans for the future is responsible, but
being petrified to make a move because you're not sure
you have all the bases covered shows little faith.

On the other hand, some are brave enough to go
ahead with their plans, but worry and fret constantly that
the worst-case scenario is inevitable. Of course, there are
others that are both Master Planners and Major Worriers
at the same time—afraid to move ahead, terrified to stay
still. In any case, faith is lacking, because the plans are
self-devised.

Then there is The Procrastinator. Yes, putting off making *any* plans is a plan in and of itself! This person's motto may be, "Ignorance is bliss." The more he pretends his reality doesn't exist, the happier and more content he is—until reality hits. That is when he tries his hand at planning and worrying, and remembers why he started procrastinating in the first place.

Whether we plan like mad, worry ourselves sick, or ignore our realities, we are attempting to exert a sense of control over what we think is our uncontrollable existence. But when we come to the end of ourselves and find no peace with our lives, perhaps then we will remember that *"the purposes of ADONAI will stand."* For all our planning, worrying or procrastinating, in the end it is ADONAI's plan that will succeed. If we trust in Him and put aside our concerns and fears, we will be able to clearly hear His voice telling us which way *He* plans to go—and then all *we* will have to do is tag along....

಄ ಄

Abba, Father, give me peace in my heart and mind. Teach me that the only kind of control to seek is self-control—to keep myself from worry and fear, and instead trust in You, knowing that You will lead me safely to my destiny. I praise You, ADONAI, for all Your purposes will stand. Show me Your ways, O God, that I may follow You all of my days in perfect peace. Help me to know that even when I can't see, You are leading me every step of the way...

We Will Be Content

"But [if we] have food and clothing—
we will be content with that." 1Timothy 6:7

I cannot believe how much money I have to lay out every month. The bare minimum I need to keep my head above water is astounding! The cost of living these days is staggering—it sends me reeling to think what would happen if I suddenly couldn't pay my bills. Throngs of collectors would appear at my front door demanding payment for services. Within a matter of weeks I would be out on the street, destitute—nothing but the clothes on my back and maybe a morsel of food. It is a miracle that anyone survives at all in this day and age, hardly able to afford life's *bare necessities.* All I can say is, thank God for air conditioning, heat, indoor plumbing, beds, bathrooms, refrigeration, electricity, computers, cell phones, satellite television, and high-speed wireless Internet access!

We have so much to be thankful for—we are blessed beyond measure. Even the poorest among us has more than those who lived just a hundred years ago, much less in the days of the apostles. The average American lifespan has almost doubled since the turn of the previous century. We have access to wondrous inventions and great medical advances—many incredible things that have raised our collective standard of living higher than ever before. One would think that we could find happiness and contentment in the marvels of modern progress… but we don't. We still want more—we want things easier, better, and less expensive.

As we sit back and ponder all the amazing comforts of life that we take for granted, we would do well to remember the words that Paul wrote in his letter to Timothy, *"[if we] have food and clothing—we will be content with that."* Paul encouraged Timothy by reminding him that we gain more when we are content with living a godly life than if we were to gain untold riches. When we focus on material things more than we dedicate ourselves to a life of godliness, we run a great risk of falling into all kinds of evil.

The disciple of Messiah is to find his contentedness in the godly life of service to the Master. Blessings abound in the life of Messiah, but we first need to learn how to see our blessings in times of need—before they are made apparent in the days of abundance. We need to recognize the source of all our blessings and provision. Indeed, if we only had food in our bellies and a garment to hide our nakedness, would we be so content?

$\approx \propto$

ADONAI, I bless Your great Name, for all blessings and provision flow from You. Lord, teach me to be content with the abundance I already have in You. Show me the true value of life's bare necessities, and make me understand that the only thing I can't live without is You. I praise You, ADONAI, Provider of food and clothing. In You alone, my King, may I be content....

They Who Are With Us

"*The servant of the man of God rose early and went out; and behold, an army [of] horse and chariot was surrounding the city. His young servant said to him, 'Oh! My master, what do we do?' And he replied, 'Fear not, for more* are *they who* are *with us than they who* are *with them.' And* אֱלִישָׁע, *'Eliysha prayed and said, 'ADONAI, I pray, open his eyes, and he will see.' And ADONAI opened the eyes of the young servant, and he saw, and behold, the hill was full of horses and chariots of fire all around* אֱלִישָׁע, *'Eliysha.*" מְלָכִים ב *M'lachiym Beit (2Kings) 6:15-17*

As disciples of Messiah, it is often a struggle for us to live as spiritual beings in a physical universe. We just can't seem to accept that the "seen" is merely a shadow of things, and the "unseen" is our true reality. It's understandably difficult to ignore that which is reasonable and logical to our minds—to accept as truth that which our senses cannot detect. But since we are now in Messiah, we have the ability to see in the spirit that which is *unseeable* with our natural eyes—and to have faith that ADONAI can be trusted implicitly, even when there is no physical evidence that He is able to do what He says.

Nowhere in the Scriptures is this truth better revealed than in this tiny glimpse into an almost trivial moment in 'Eliysha's life. All too often, we are just like 'Eliysha's servant—we have difficulty seeing that all around us is the invisible army of God. But regardless of what we see with our eyes, the *reality* of our walk with Yeshua is this: *"Fear not, for more* are *they who* are *with us than they who* are *with them..."*

There is no reason for us to run and hide when the enemy comes at us with his legions! It's funny how we are quick to see devils around every corner, but spiritual armies are far outside our field of vision. When the devil says "Boo!" we scurry behind the nearest rock—when *in reality* we are surrounded by an army of ADONAI, prepared to fight in our defense. The enemy already knows that cavalry is there, yet he is able to manipulate and dupe us because we don't really believe it ourselves. So *"stand up against the devil, and he will flee from you."* Why? Because there just might be an army of the Lord over your shoulder!

ও৵ ৶৹

Mighty God, King Messiah, Leader of heavenly armies, I believe You have surrounded me and will protect me from all my enemies. ADONAI, teach me to stand firm without fear; open Your servant's eyes, that I may see the mountain covered with horses and fiery chariots. Help me to see Your reality with 20/20 vision —that I may not trust what I perceive, but what is imperceptible to my natural eyes. Deliverer, Redeemer, my whole faith is in You. I praise You and worship You for Your awesome, invisible power....

The Purpose of Man

"Furthermore, from these, my son, be warned: the making of many books has no end, and much study wearies the flesh. The end of the whole matter let us hear: 'Fear God and keep His commands, for this is the whole [purpose] of man.'" קֹהֶלֶת *Kohelet (Ecclesiastes) 12:12-13*

What if every time the doors of your congregation open, you are there—twice, three times, maybe even four times a week—sitting in the front row, ready to hear the Word? What if you also attend a weekly Bible study? What if you buy a new faith-related book every week and devour it? What if every day, you spend two or three hours just studying the Word? What if you write and publish an entire daily devotional book?

What if you do all these things, and...

... you never lead someone to Messiah...

... you never have peace or joy...

... you never make a difference in other peoples' lives...

... you never learn how to give or receive love...

... you take your spouse or children for granted or treat them poorly...

... you continually have bouts with depression...

… your life never really changes…

For teachers and students alike, the trap is the same: write or read more books, and you will grow in Messiah. Teach or study the Scriptures more, and you will know God better. It's just not true. Read all you want, study all you want, espouse knowledge all you want, but it won't make an ounce of difference in the end. Unless…

Unless we *"fear God and keep His commands."*

Knowing what the Word of God says is not the point. The point is *doing* what He wants us to do—putting what we have learned into action. And what does He want us to do? Change. He wants us to change, and then facilitate change in others. He wants us to grow up in our salvation and lead others to do the same. Staying up until all hours of the night, neglecting our spouse and family while we study the Scriptures? *"[It] has no end, and much study wearies the flesh."* No, we already know what we need to do—so let's do it.

And *"the end of the whole matter"* is this: *"Fear God and keep His commands, for this is the whole [purpose] of man."*

క్రా ఆఠ

Father, help me to do more than sit here and silently read this prayer today. Pick me up, if You have to, and get me on my face, that I may bow down and give You the reverence You deserve. Lift up my hands, if You must, and let shouts of praise come from my lips. Teach me, Father, to stop amassing knowledge without allowing it to bring forth actions of faith and love. I bless You, ADONAI. I praise You, my King! Show me Your ways, and I will follow You with *all* that I am….

There Is a Future

*"Do not let your heart be envious of sinners,
but [be] in the fear of ADONAI all the day. For
there is a future [for you], and your hope will not
be cut off."* מִשְׁלֵי *Mish'lei (Proverbs) 23:17-18*

The way of the wicked often appears to be one of
glamour, success, prosperity—even favor. Through the
eyes of jealousy, we see the sinner surrounded by people
who freely offer adoration, devotion, esteem, *money....*
Envy causes us to be drawn in—to covet the methods
and charisma of the unrighteous—because in our minds,
the ends justify the means. Surely if blessing is the result,
then the means by which that blessing was acquired is
just.

Not on your life!

This is a theme that permeates the Scriptures. The
righteous look upon the wicked and yearn for a mere
morsel of their wealth and success. Yet the Word's only
consolation is, "Don't worry, they'll get theirs! You have
life—they will only reap death and destruction. They
may be happy now, but you'll be happiest in the end.
Hang in there!"

For some reason, that's just not good enough for us.
"Hey, eternal life and future rewards are great, but I want
my blessing now, now, now! Why do the sinners and the
wicked get all the happiness and success? I'm serving You,
Lord—why don't *I* get the blessing? Why do *I* have to
struggle, while it's so easy for *them*? I have a lot to offer,

too, You know. Why don't *I* get any of that attention? Those horrible people—I *deserve* what they *have!*"

In case you couldn't place the voice, that was your flesh talking. Why does the flesh react with such envy? Because all the possessions of the wicked are things of the flesh, and the flesh naturally wants its own. But contrary to the desires of our flesh, our spirit has been given new life—and *it* only wants the things of God. Worldly success and prosperity are not indicators of God's favor. In fact, *"Better is the little of the righteous, than the abundance of many wicked."* (Psalm 37:16)

"Do not let your heart be envious of sinners, but [be] in the fear of ADONAI...*"* Why? Because the days of the wicked will be cut short, but we have a future! The righteous possess the greatest treasure of all: hope. We know from where our provision comes, we know where our future lies, and we can place our hope and trust in the One whose plans *always* succeed.

გა ჯა

ADONAI, thank You for setting me free from being envious of the unrighteous. I praise You for releasing me from the desires of my flesh, and for reminding me of the abundant rewards I have already received in You. Teach me, O God, the ways of the one who fears You. I bless You, Father, for You truly do heal the heart and mind, and You give much hope for the future....

Come After Me

"If anyone comes to me, and does not hate his own father, and mother, and life, and children, and brothers, and sisters, and yet even his own life, he is not able to be my disciple; and whoever does not bear his [execution] stake, and come after me, is not able to be my disciple."
Luke 14:26-27

Hate your family to follow Yeshua. Hate... that's a pretty strong word—did Yeshua actually say to hate your own family? Indeed, the Master really does teach us to hate our families... but He tells us to hate our *own lives* as well.

Our minds are capable of understanding many different kinds of love—we love our families, but we also love a good pizza—yet when it comes to hate, we have a hard time seeing its subtle shades. Yeshua doesn't use this language to exaggerate, but to be emphatic about the seriousness of putting the Kingdom first—truly first. Yeshua is not teaching the alienation of one's family, but the price we must be willing to pay when we embrace the Good News—that there is a real cost of discipleship.

However, we must be careful to not confuse the cost of discipleship with "sacrifice for the ministry." We are not called to put ministry to others above ministry to our own families. We cannot neglect our spouse for days on end because someone else is in need—this is not the kind of sacrifice the Master requires of us. When we pay the cost of discipleship, it is a price that we pay with our *own* lives—not with the lives of our loved ones. Paying the cost of discipleship is for the Kingdom, and the Master does not set a price that is more than we can truly afford.

The real cost of discipleship—the price we truly must pay in order to follow Yeshua—is simply that we follow nothing and no one else. Not our spouses, our families, or our friends... and certainly not ourselves. The cost of discipleship is our freedom—we give up all rights to our own lives.

And yet, once we have enslaved our lives to Yeshua, we realize that He has given us a *new* freedom—and this is *true* freedom. The freedom to bear our own burdens is taken away, and we discover that the execution-stake we are carrying is not that heavy at all.

ॐ ✦

Yeshua, I renounce all rights to my life in order that I may follow You. Everything in this world is a distant second to You. ADONAI, I thank You that when I give myself completely to You, I can expect blessings without measure. My spouse is a blessing, my parents are a blessing, my children are a blessing, my job is a blessing —yet I give them up to You as well. Help me to be more devoted to You every day. Thank You for this incredible freedom that You have given to me, my Master....

What Smells?

"And to God be thanks, who at all times is leading us in triumph in the Messiah, and He is manifesting through us in every place the fragrance of knowing Him. Because of Messiah, we are an aroma to God, among those being saved and among those being destroyed. To the one, indeed, a fragrance of death [leading] to death, and to the other, a fragrance of life [leading] to life. And for these things, who is sufficient?" 2Corinthians 2:14-16

The aroma of salvation is absolute, distinct, unmistakable—and yet, salvation is often perceived in such relative terms that no two people *smell* it the same. How can it be that to one it smells as sweet as flowers, and to another it stinks like sewage? Our salvation is *"an aroma to God"*—to those being saved it is *"a fragrance of life,"* but to the sinner, *"a fragrance of death."*

As disciples of Messiah, our olfactory nerves have been spiritually recreated so that we can now smell salvation for what it truly is. Yet we still war with our flesh, which can easily manipulate our senses. To our own nostrils, the fragrance of our salvation becomes polluted, and the stench of our former ways is deceptively covered over. Why else do we fall back into sin, except that it seems pleasing to us at the time? We are fooled into believing that doing evil is "sinfully delicious," and that Life in the Messiah smells like the pit of hell.

So what do *you* smell like today? As ambassadors of Messiah, we have a responsibility for representing Him to the lost. It's one thing if a sinner can't smell the sweetness of the Savior because he can't detect the difference between flowers and fertilizer, but it's another thing altogether if the ambassador stinks to high heaven! Have you been spending your time digging in the dirt, or are you clean and presentable, perfumed in holiness, godliness and purity? If we are living in such a way as to erect obstacles that will keep *"those being destroyed"* from the Lord, in whose lap will the blame be laid? But if we are living in such a way that will cause the aroma of God to permeate the sinner's senses, on whose head will be the glory?

When ADONAI regenerates the snout of a false-smelling soul, let us be the first fragrance to please his nostrils. Let us strive to be anointed with the scent of righteousness, to lead the formerly senseless to the aromatic gardens of glory. As we purify ourselves, let us not contribute to the foul stink of death, but manifest *"in every place the fragrance of knowing Him."*

ෙ ෙ

ADONAI, wash me clean, that I will smell of righteousness and not the filth of my former self. I am new! I am cleansed! Make my purity a perfume for the lost, that my aroma will be pleasing to the senses and lead others from a path of sin to the road of life. Father, thank You for immersing me in your Spirit and anointing me with the fragrance of the Good News. I savor the sweetness of Your salvation....

The Joyful Shout

"O the happiness of the people [who]
know the [joyful] shout! O ADONAI, in the
light of Your face they walk habitually. In
Your Name they rejoice all the day, and in
Your righteousness they are exalted. For the
splendor of their strength is You, and by Your
favor does our strength increase. For ADONAI
is our shield, and of the Holy One of יִשְׂרָאֵל,
Yis'rael, our King." תְּהִלִּים *T'hillim (Psalms)*
89:15-18

In the world of the Scriptures, man responds to the
spiritual work of ADONAI with action. As the Body of
Messiah has historically grown away from its Scriptural
roots, however, spirituality has been rerouted into the
reservoir of the mind, unable to escape. Trapped within,
spirituality then manifests itself as intellectual titillation
at one extreme, or ineffectual emotion on the other. But
primarily, it has resulted in a Body that is generally
lifeless and neutral.

Happiness in the context of the Scriptures defines
a lifestyle of contentment, fulfillment, blessings, and
abundance. The Psalmist tells us that happy people
"know the [joyful] shout." And what is this shout? It is
the literal, physical response to walking *"in the light of"*
ADONAI's presence. It comes from the joy that we have
in being exalted by His righteousness.

Is this the mindless shout of emotionalism? Is it the
metaphoric shout of intellectualism? No, it is a shout of

praise! Only in the presence of ADONAI can joy truly be made known and the praises of ADONAI proclaimed. From where does our happiness come? How does our strength increase? By the favor of ADONAI! When we live to please Him, He gives us our strength and shield, in which we glory.

The presence of ADONAI is as real and tangible as flesh and blood—and it produces actual and physical responses in our lives. We are not happy *because* we know the joyful shout, but because we know the One who we celebrate and in whose presence we rejoice. This is not the joy of our imaginations, or the happiness of our own creation. The joyful shout has body and presence, it is physical and audible—and it is our real response to a spiritual God.

ॐ ॐ

ADONAI, release me from the prison of my mind and the inhibitions of religiosity, and teach me to let Your praises come forth boldly from my mouth. In all circumstances, Abba, Father, let me praise You with my lips and shout for all who have ears, that they may hear of Your wonders. I bless Your name, for You are not an idea in my mind or a fantasy in my head, but You are the living God, real and true, exalted One...

Suddenly Broken

"A man [who] becomes stiff-necked [after] much rebuke will be suddenly broken, and there will be no healing." מִשְׁלֵי *Mish'lei (Proverbs) 29:1*

We all need to be put in our place every once in a while—some of us more often than others. But the fact that we deserve a good rebuke from time to time doesn't mean that we are evil, immoral people. Rebuke is not just for sinners—it is also for the righteous when we are lulled back into our old ways and need to be slapped to our senses... revived from a temporary slip into insanity. A good rebuke helps to get us back on the path toward Messiah.

We ought to realize that there is something wrong when we begin to resent godly correction. Perhaps we start to feel as if we're being corrected just a *little* too often by the *same* person about the *same* issue—over, and over, and over again. Is it possible for rebuke to turn into abuse? Certainly. But before we jump to that conclusion, maybe we should instead be on our faces before the Master. We should allow the persistent rebuke to do its work in our lives—without regard for the one rebuking and whatever his intentions may be.

When rebuke comes, no matter what we think of it, the last thing we should do is resist, for the *"man [who] becomes stiff-necked [after] much rebuke will be suddenly broken..."* We need to remember that ADONAI uses godly rebuke to fashion us after Messiah, and we must always remain pliable in His hands. If we harden ourselves to rebuke, *"there will be no healing,"* because rebuke naturally comes with much force and power. If we are unable to bend under the stress, we will surely snap in two from its unrelenting strength.

True correction is from ADONAI. Though we usually will not like it, we must fight the temptation to reject it—all the more when we think we don't deserve it… and *especially* if we think we don't deserve it from the one dishing it out! The more *pummeling* that is applied to us, the more *pliable* we need to become. The more we dislike the rebuker, the more we need to cultivate humility and love in our hearts.

When rebuke is from the Lord, it has the power to break us; but if we receive it correctly, it has the power to *change* us. We need to remember that everything from ADONAI is done in His love, so we can trust that whatever He causes or allows will enable us to grow—as long as we refuse to get in the way….

ಶೃ ೞ

Father, I want to change. Teach me how to bend with correction, instead of rigidly resisting it and risking permanent brokenness. Abba, I trust You with all my heart, and I praise You for Your most excellent ways! Thank You, ADONAI, for loving me enough to bring correction into my life, and for not letting me continue in my own ways. I bless Your Name—I am in Your hands….

Is This the Messiah?

"Come, see a man who told me all things—as many as I [ever] did! Is this the Messiah?" יוֹחָנָן *Yochanan (John) 4:29*

When she arrived at Ya'akov's well to draw water that day, the Samaritan woman did not expect to leave without her water jar. She never imagined that a Jew resting by the well would have anything to do with her, much less offer *her* a drink from the spring of eternal life. She soon forgot all about her container and the thirst that went with it—for now she had met Yeshua, and she realized she would never be thirsty again.

The story of the Samaritan woman ought to remind us of a very important truth: that even though the Master can reach us in the most common places, there is nothing *commonplace* about a life-changing encounter with Yeshua. And yet these days, we rarely see this kind of response to Him—a response like the Samaritan woman exhibited when she finally realized that she had met the One who was to come. For some reason, we fail to be amazed with Him anymore, and the miraculous ways of Messiah are now just everyday events.

But maybe there is something else at work here. Maybe we are not amazed when someone gets healed or receives salvation because we are still questioning. We hear the testimony of miracles here, witness an amazing feat there—but we walk away asking, *"Is this the Messiah?"* Perhaps we are not asking with the same incredulous hope that the Samaritan woman had. Perhaps we are asking with doubt in our hearts, because we have not yet had that life-changing experience ourselves...

The Samaritan woman was transformed because she met a man who told her everything she ever did. The Master was able to reach her where no one else could— He saw in her things that no one else could see. Today, disciple of Messiah, we need to grab our water jars and head for the well. We need to expect that our containers will be too small to hold what will be waiting for us when we get there. Run to the well, disciple of Messiah, but not with the hope that you will drink—run with the hope that you will be filled, and will thirst no more....

એ એ

ADONAI, I am running to the well today—I am dry and thirsty because I have been waiting for You to come. Take the doubt and fear from my heart, Lord, that I may know the answer to my question: the One who knows me, and all that I have done—He *is* Messiah! I praise You, O God, for from You alone flow the well-springs of eternal life. Once and for all, Master, fill me, that I may return from the well with more than my jar could ever hold...

Piece of Wood

"Every man is [a senseless] brute without knowledge; every goldsmith is put to shame by the idol [he fashions]. For false is his molten image, and there is no רוּחַ, *ruach in them. They are worthless, [the] work of those in error—in the time of their inspection, they [will] perish. Not like these is the Portion of* יַעֲקֹב, *Ya'akov, for He is [the] maker of all things. And* יִשְׂרָאֵל, *Yis'rael is the rod of His inheritance—*יהוה צְבָאוֹת, ADONAI *Tz'vaot is His name."* יִרְמְיָהוּ *Yir'm'yahu (Jeremiah) 10:14-17*

"Hey, Stupid! It's just a piece of wood!" is the prophet's sobering cry. An idol fashioned by human hands—how can it possibly have the power to save? And yet, we create false idols, we carve and mold our own gods, and we bow down to them. Why? Because *"every man is [a senseless] brute without knowledge"*—in other words, we're *stupid.* Indeed, we must be *complete idiots* to think that we will be saved by the work of our own hands.

"Every goldsmith is put to shame by the idol [he fashions]." Each of us has had a hand in the creation of our own false idols. Perhaps they are idols of wood or gold; perhaps they are emotional, spiritual, or even financial gods that we have fashioned and served. But every idol of any image is false—it does not live, nor does it give life. Our idols are devoid of spirit and

worth, and *"in the time of their inspection, they [will] perish"*—and us along with them.

But *"not like these* is *the Portion of Ya'akov"*! ADONAI, the God of Yis'rael—in Him is unending worth, and everlasting life. He is not a lifeless, metal god that we can melt down and sell for money when we are poor; nor is he a dead hunk of lumber that we can hack up and burn for heat when we are cold. He is not made in the mind, nor by the hands of men—it is men *He* has made, *"for He is [the] maker of all things."*

No force on earth, no notion in our heads, no tool of our own formation, no false idol to which we are enslaved—none of them can save us; *"they* are *worthless, [the] work of those in error."* Only One alone—the Maker of all things—can deliver us, and He is worthy of the devotion of His creation. We are *"[senseless] brutes"* to elevate and trust in our own works and plans over those of the Maker. There is no one else like the Portion of Ya'akov—He alone is the Creator. ADONAI Tz'vaot is His name…

ও ৬

ADONAI Tz'vaot, You are God—You alone. Teach me to no longer put my trust in a faith of my own making, but instead to have faith only in You. Show me the error of my idolatry, that I may burn up all things which I have made and followed, and instead follow only You. I praise You, O Portion of Ya'akov—reform me according to Your ways, that I may follow You, Maker of all things…

When Lack Is Gain

"A Psalm of דָּוִד, David. ADONAI is *my* shepherd, I do not lack; In pastures of tender grass He causes me to lie down; By quiet waters He leads me. My soul He refreshes; He leads me in paths of righteousness, For His name's sake, Also—when I walk in a valley of death-shadow, I fear no evil, for You are *with* me; Your rod and Your staff—they comfort me. You arrange before me a table, in front of my adversaries, You have anointed my head with oil, my cup is full! Only—goodness and loving-kindness pursue me, All the days of my life, And my dwelling is in the house of ADONAI, For the length of [all my] days."
תְּהִלִּם *T'hillim (Psalms) 23*

This Psalm of David rests on a single thought: "*ADONAI is my shepherd.*" This is true whether we choose to be shepherded or not—it is our choice to stray or stay. Yet to receive the benefits of His shepherding, we must *allow* ourselves to be led—fully submitted, listening only to the sound of His voice. Once we embrace this relationship and it ceases to be one-sided (with ADONAI constantly pursuing us as we go our *own* way), the immediate result is complete fulfillment: "*I do not lack.*"

Often we are confused by this, thinking that by lacking nothing, we will no longer experience the effects of life, trials and struggles. But this is not the case. It is true that in lacking nothing, we have rest, serenity, guidance, and restoration of our inner person—and these things are given to us for Heaven's sake. Why? Because there *will* be *"death-shadows"* over our lives, there *will* be *"evil"* set against us. Yet in ADONAI we *"do not lack"*—we have access to the continual presence of the Shepherd, the One whom we need in order to make it through those times of *"death-shadow."* We have no fear because we see our Shepherd's rod and staff before us, and we rest assured: He is here.

Under the care of our Shepherd, *"goodness and loving-kindness will pursue [us] all the days of [our] life."* Since we will not be without troubles, our prayer should be that we will not be without *God.* Submitting every-thing to ADONAI brings total peace, even in the face of adversity and troubles. In Yeshua we gain the greatest possession of all: a total lack... of nothing.

ॐ ॐ

ADONAI, Father, lead me, restore me, guide me—I receive You anew today as my Shepherd, the one voice to whom I will listen. Forgive me for trying to find Your peace, comfort, and direction by going my own way. Thank You, O God, for the eternal rest that I am able to have in You today, right now. I praise You, ADONAI, for the assurance You bring as You go before me—leading me, guiding me, and shepherding me along Your perfect way....

Loss of All Things

> *"But what things were to my gain, these I have counted—because of Messiah—loss. Yes, indeed, and I count all things to be loss, because of the excellency of the knowledge of Messiah Yeshua my Master, because of whom I suffered loss of all things, and consider them to be excrement, that I may gain Messiah, and be found in Him..." Philippians 3:7-8*

Because of Messiah, we gain much liberty and joy, peace and well-being. More than that, we gain the hope of our salvation, even from death. Yeshua has given abundantly of Himself for us, that we might gain more of Him in our lives. But in exchange for all that we gain, what are we willing to lose? Do we even believe that there are things we must be willing to give up in order to gain Messiah?

Many of us are not really willing to consider this idea. We have our salvation now, and that is all well and good... but certainly, there is more to life than being "in Messiah." After all, we think, there are areas of life where we can't realistically count on Yeshua to help. We need medicine to maintain our health, we need more money to pay our bills, we need more recognition to advance in our careers. We have to wear the right clothes, know the right people, and own the newest stuff. But with such confidence in the flesh, we fail to realize that *"because of the excellency of the knowledge of Messiah Yeshua,"* our salvation extends to every area of life.

Gaining Messiah is not about ignoring our practical needs; it is about giving up—losing—all reliance on ourselves to meet those needs. Our success in life does not depend on how much we gain, but on how much we *lose* for the sake of Messiah Yeshua. The things that *"were to [our] gain"* are worthless, without any power whatsoever. Paul goes so far as to *"consider them to be excrement"* —everything is an utter waste, compared to gaining Messiah.

To gain Messiah, we must suffer the loss of ourselves —the confidence in our abilities, talents or circumstances to deliver us from the crises of life. When we *"count all things to be loss,"* it is an affirmation that we owe our very lives to the One who paid the debt on our behalf—and only in Him do we truly gain anything at all. Indeed, it is only in the loss of ourselves that we can *"be found in Him..."*

ঔ ৺

Abba, Father, today I lose myself, that I may gain Messiah. Teach me, ADONAI, to lose confidence in myself and my abilities, and to put all my hope and trust in You. Father, show me how to relinquish control and to allow myself to suffer the loss of all things, so that I will gain life only in You. I bless You, ADONAI, for finding me when I was lost, and for teaching me even now how to lose myself in You all over again...

As People Come In

"And they come in to you, [Y'chez'ke-el,]
as people [usually] come in, and they sit before
you—My people. And [they] hear your words,
but they [do] not do them. For with their
mouths they make [declarations of] love, [but]
their hearts are going after dishonest gain. And
behold, you are to them like a singer of love
[songs—just] a pleasant voice, and [one who]
plays well on an instrument. For they have heard
your words, but they are not doing them."
יְחֶזְקֵאל Y'chez'ke-el (Ezekiel) 33:31-32

What would it be like if we could see ourselves
from the perspectives of our congregational leaders
and musicians? As they face us—the congregation—
what do they see? Perhaps they see us hanging on their
every word as they teach from the Scriptures. Maybe
they see us enthralled in the throes of worship as they
sing and play their instruments. Perhaps they see a
change in us—perhaps not. They see us walk out the
door, and then at the next meeting they see us coming
back for more. Do you think they wonder if their
ministry has had any effect on us at all?

For Y'chez'ke-el, his "congregants" were not showing
up for the way his ministry impacted their lives—they
came strictly for the entertainment value. To them, he
was there for their enjoyment, "like a singer of love [songs
—just] a pleasant voice." They took pleasure in the performance—in his fervent, passionate display and his

precise, well-executed oration—like sitting before one who *"plays well on an instrument."* They participated in the show by responding with *"[declarations of] love"* to ADONAI... but in their hearts they had only the desire for *"dishonest gain."*

Do we attend our congregational meetings with motives that are any different? Think about how we determine if we've had a good meeting: we enjoyed the message, we enjoyed the music, we were moved to tears or laughter, we felt like we were touched by God. The fact of the matter is that all these things can also happen while watching a really good *movie*—it's all subjective.

Our walk as disciples of Messiah must be far more than seeking spiritual experiences as a form of entertainment. Just think how our lives would change if we measured the quality of our congregational meetings, not by how much we enjoy them or feel that "God showed up," but by how our lives are affected, changed —and then *stay* that way? Let us stop making *"[declarations of] love"* with our mouths, and start *demonstrating* that love with our feet and our hands. We need to do more than simply hear His words, but take them to heart and *do* them....

ADONAI, I bless Your Name, for You speak Your Word of truth to me... even when I'm not listening. Abba, teach me to not only hear Your Word, but to *do* it—to stop seeking You just through an "experience," but to fervently seek You through the *evidence* that my life has been forever changed. I praise You, O God, for You are willing and able to change me if I will just give You the chance...

With Him No More

> *"…therefore, many of [Yeshua's] disciples having heard [His teaching], said, 'This word is hard; who is able to hear [and accept] it?' And Yeshua, having known in Himself that His disciples were murmuring about this, said to them, 'Does this [strike you as scandalous and] cause you to stumble?' …From this time [on], many of His disciples went away backward, and were walking with Him no more."*
> יוֹחָנָן *Yochanan (John) 6:60-61, 66*

They walked with Him. They talked with Him. They touched Him and saw His face. They beheld His miracles and felt the presence of His authority. They broke bread with Him and sat at His feet as they listened to His teachings—the very words that could change their lives.

It is hard to imagine turning away from the One whom each of us longs to behold. I would be the first to give up all I have, in order to be—even just for a few moments—in the presence of my Master.

Or would I?

One day, the Master was teaching His disciples that if anyone was to have eternal life, He needed to eat the Master's flesh and drink His blood. To this, some disciples responded, *"How is this one able to give us his flesh to eat?"* —they didn't understand (vs. 52). Others murmured among themselves, *"This word is hard; who is able to*

hear it?"—they couldn't accept. So *"from this* time *[on],
many of His disciples"*—many of them—*"went away
backward, and were walking with Him no more."*

It is inconceivable that anyone who has been in the
very presence of the Master could even have the strength,
much less the will, to turn away from Him. Surely, there
must have been something innately undeniable about
Him that would draw people in, causing them to devote
their lives to Him and His ways.

But it didn't happen that way at all. In fact, people
left Him—*many* people—and returned to their own
ways. To them, His teachings were just too hard.

The Master is asking us today, *"Do you also wish
to go away?"* (vs. 67) Are we such dedicated, devoted
disciples of Messiah that we would keep holding fast
even if He spoke a hard word to us? Indeed, which of
His words are *not* hard? Which of His teachings does
not cause us to stumble when we walk according to our
own ways, rather than His? Is there anything at all about
Messiah that does not appear scandalous to those who
do not understand His ways?

Would I walk with my Master even when no one
else would? I hope so.

I bless Your Name, my Master. Lord, give me ears
to hear; speak hard words to me, that I may change and
become more like You. O God, let me see Your face,
that I may know You and hold fast to Your ways. I give
You all the glory, honor and praise, my Master, and I
will walk with You alone for the rest of my days....

Glossary

This reverse glossary is alphabetized according to the transliterated English found throughout the devotionals. Each glossary entry includes the Hebrew, transliteration, and English translation or definition. Below is a pronunciation key to assist the reader with verbalization of the English transliterations.

Pronunciation Key			
a = "ah"	*e* = "eh"	*i* = "ee"	*o* = "oh"
u = "oo"	*ch* = guttural sound in back of throat, as in *"Bach"* or *"loch,"* not "ch" as in *"much"*		

אַחְאָב	Ach'av	Ahab
אֲחַזְיָהוּ	'Achaz'yahu	Ahaziah
יהוה	ADONAI	The "Sacred Name" of God, YHVH, represented by the substitution "Adonai" in all capital letters. (See Introduction for more information.)
אֲדֹנָי	Adonai	Lord, Master
אֲדֹנָי יהוה	*Adonai ELOHIYM*	Sovereign Lord, Lord God

א	alef	First; first letter of the Hebrew Alphabet
אָמֵן	amen	Truly, so be it
עָמוֹס	Amos	Amos
אַבְרָהָם	Av'raham	Abraham
אַיָּלוֹן	Ayalon	Aijalon
בַּעַל	Baal	Baal
ב	Beit	Second; second letter of the Hebrew alphabet
חַנָּה	Chanah	Hannah
חֲנַנְיָה	'Chanan'yah	Hananiah
חֲנוֹךְ	'Chanok	Enoch
חָסִיד	Chasiyd	Holy Ones
כֹּהֵן	cohen	priest
דָּן	Dan	Dan
דָּנִיֵּאל	Daniyel	Daniel
דָּוִד	David	David
עֵלִי	Eliy	Eli
אֵלִיָּהוּ	Eliyahu	Elijah
אֱלִישָׁע	'Eliysha	Elisha
עֶלְיוֹן	El'yon	High; (The) Most High
אֱמֹרִי	'Emoriy	Amorites
אֶתְפַּתַּח	et'patach	The Aramaic that underscores Εφφαθα, *Ephphatha*, "Be opened!"
גִּבְעוֹן	Giv'on	Gideon
הַלְלוּ יָהּ	Hal'lu Yah	hallelujah, Praise Yah
הַשָּׂטָן	HaSatan	the Adversary, Satan
הֶבֶל	Hevel	Abel
עִבְרִים	Iv'riym	Hebrews
אִיּוֹב	Iyov	Job
אִיזֶבֶל	Iyzevel	Jezebel

כֵּיפָא	Keifa	Cephas / Peter
כִּנֶּרֶת	Kineret	Gennesaret, that is, the Sea of Galilee
קֹהֶלֶת	Kohelet	preacher, teacher; a possible pseudonym for Solomon
לְבָנוֹן	L'vanon	Lebanon
מְלָכִים	M'lachiym	Kings
מָשִׁיחַ	Mashiyach	Messiah, meaning, "anointed one." In Greek, Χριστός, Christos (Christ)
מַתִּתְיָהוּ	Matit'yahu	Matthew
מִדְיָן	Mid'yan	Midian
מִשְׁלֵי	Mish'lei	Proverbs
מְלֶכֶת הַשָּׁמַיִם	M'lechet HaShamayim	Literally, Queen [of] the Heavens. A reference to the collection of celestial bodies, including the sun, moon and stars.
מֹשֶׁה	Moshe	Moses
נְתַנְאֵל	N'tan'el	Nathaniel
נְבָט	N'vat	Nebat
נָתָן	Natan	Nathan
נֹחַ	Noach	Noah
רַבִּי	Rabbi	Rabbi, Teacher
רוּחַ	ruach	spirit
רוּחַ הַקֹּדֶשׁ	Ruach HaKodesh	The Holy Spirit
שְׁלֹמֹה	Sh'lomoh	Solomon
שְׁמוּאֵל	Sh'muel	Samuel
שְׁאוֹל	Sh'ol	(The) grave
שַׁבָּת	Shabbat	Sabbath

שָׁלוֹם	shalom	peace, wholeness
שִׁמְעוֹן	Shim'on	Simon
שֹׁפְטִים	Shof'tiym	Judges
סֶלָה	selah	to lift up, exalt; possibly a musical term indicating a pause or interruption
תְּהִלִּם	T'hillim	Psalms
תּוֹרָה	Torah	Instruction, teaching, referring to the five books of Moses. Translated incorrectly in English as "Law."
צְבָאוֹת	Tz'vaot	armies, hosts
צִיּוֹן	Tziyon	Zion
יְחֶזְקֵאל	Y'chez'ke-el	Ezekiel
יְהוֹשֻׁעַ	Y'hoshua	Joshua; "Yah is my salvation"
יְהוּדָה	Y'hudah	Judah
יְשַׁעְיָהוּ	Y'sha'yahu	Isaiah
יַעֲקֹב	Ya'akov	Jacob, James
יָה	Yah	Jah; shortened form of the "Sacred Name"
יָרָבְעָם	Yarav'am	Jeroboam
יֵהוּא	Yehu	Jehu
יֵשׁוּעַ	Yeshua	salvation
יִרְמְיָהוּ	Yir'm'yahu	Jeremiah
יִשְׂרָאֵל	Yis'rael	Israel
יִצְחָק	Yitz'chak	Isaac
יוֹחָנָן	Yochanan	John
יוֹסֵף	Yosef	Joseph

About the Author

Kevin Geoffrey, born Kevin Geoffrey Berger, is the firstborn son of a first-generation American, non-religious, secular Jewish family. From childhood, he was ashamed of his Jewish heritage, deliberately attempting to hide his identity as a Jew. Kevin spent his youth like most Jewish kids—essentially assimilated into American culture, embracing the things of the world and pursuing the things of the flesh.

At fifteen years old, Kevin was diagnosed with Crohn's disease, a serious and incurable disorder of the digestive tract. After experiencing a sudden and apparently miraculous healing, Kevin's heart was opened to consider the possibility of something in which he had always been taught not to believe: the existence of God. A few years later, through various influential encounters and relationships, Kevin accepted Yeshua as Messiah and became what he then understood as a "born-again Christian."

Upon graduating from high school, Kevin rejected higher learning to half-heartedly pursue a career in music. With delusions of grandeur and his newfound identity as a "Christian," Kevin legally changed his name to Kevin Geoffrey, completing his assimilation from "Jew" to "Christian." When his ambition as a "rock star" ultimately failed to materialize, Kevin conceded defeat and entered Jacksonville University (Florida), where he graduated with high honors.

Throughout college, Kevin zealously studied the Scriptures. Seeking like-minded believers, he visited several Christian churches, but he was unable to find a place to call home. It was during this time that Kevin revealed his Jewish heritage to a close friend, who introduced him to the existence of the Messianic Jewish Movement.

Shortly before meeting his soon-to-be wife Esther, Kevin became part of a non-denominational Christian Fellowship where he was discipled in his faith, as well as in praise and worship ministry. Together, Kevin and Esther continued to learn about the Messianic Jewish Movement and became occasional attendees at the local Messianic congregation. Within a year and a half, and after the Christian Fellowship suffered a devastating split, Kevin was able to fully embrace his call as a Messianic Jew and was restored to his Jewish heritage.

Today, Kevin is a strong advocate for the restoration of Jewish believers in Yeshua to their distinct calling and identity as the remnant of Israel. He is a husband, a father, and also the principal laborer of Perfect Word Ministries, a Messianic Jewish equipping ministry. To date, Kevin has authored six books, including those in the Messianic Devotional, Preparing the Way *inPrint*, and The Messianic Life series. He is also a regular contributor to *Jewish Voice Today* magazine.

Kevin has been licensed as a Messianic Jewish Teacher by the IAMCS (International Alliance of Messianic Congregations and Synagogues), and ordained by Jewish Voice Ministries International (JVMI). He has taught in live seminars and conferences throughout the United States, as well as multiple Messianic congregations and synagogues. He has also served in congregational leadership, and as an anointed praise and worship leader both in congregations and in regional, national and international Messianic conferences.

Kevin resides in Phoenix, Arizona with his wife Esther and their three beautiful sons, Isaac, Josiah and Hosea.

A MESSIANIC JEWISH EQUIPPING MINISTRY

Calling the Body of Messiah to maturity
by teaching the simple application of Scripture
for a radically changed life in Yeshua

www.PerfectWordMinistries.org

about perfect word • teachings • order resources • join our list • donate

Other Books by Kevin Geoffrey

Deny Yourself: The Atoning Command of Yom Kippur

Giving ADONAI His Due: Praise and Worship (forthcoming)

Messianic Daily Devotional

Messianic Mo'adiym Devotional

Messianic Torah Devotional

The Messianic Life: Bearing the Fruit of the Spirit (forthcoming)

The Messianic Life: Being a Disciple of Messiah

The Real Story of Chanukah: Dedicated to the Death

Comments? Questions? Ask Kevin!

kevin@perfect-word.org • 1-888-321-PWMI • PO BOX 82954 Phoenix AZ 85071